40 Years in the Desert
Temple Sinai Cookbook

A Collection of Recipes by
Temple Sinai Reform Congregation
3405 Gulling Road
Reno, Nevada 89503
Phone: (775) 747-5508
Fax: (775) 747-1911
EMail: Temple.Sinai@Juno.com

Religious School Illustrators
Aaron S., age 9
Adam C., age 12
Alex K., age 12
Anna L., age 12
Arielle S., age 12
Ben L., age 8
Carly G., age 12
Chloe N., age 8
David S., age 12
Elizabeth T., age 9
Eva M., age 9
Greg L., age 9
Jack D., age 8
Joe H., age 12
Jonathan C., age 10
Leah W., age 9
Royce F., age 12
Sam D., age 12
Stefan K., age 12

Cover Photo by Steve Davis ©2004 Steve Davis
Holiday Text by Adrienne Tropp ©2004 Adrienne Tropp
Copyright ©2004 Temple Sinai

Published by STI
Reno, Nevada

ISBN: 1-880815-17-6

Printed in the United States of America
by Maverick Publications
Bend, Oregon

Dedication

To commemorate Temple Sinai's fortieth year in the high desert of Reno, Nevada, the Sisterhood has compiled this book. Temple Sinai was formed in 1962, holding services in rented facilities until 1970 when the Gulling Road facility was built. In 1990 the building was expanded to include classrooms. The congregation has since outgrown its facilities. In 2001 a Building Fund Campaign began for a new building. Proceeds from this cookbook will go to the Building Fund and the Religious School. This cookbook is dedicated to our loyal members and friends.

Acknowledgment

We have many people to thank in putting this cookbook together. Temple Sinai's first cookbook, "Temple Sinai's Jewish Fest 1998 Congregational Cookbook, Volume I – Holidays" was spearheaded by Zoe Rose and Nadine Lipson. The second cookbook "Feasts for All Seasons. Temple Sinai Celebrates, Volume 2" was coordinated by Sharon Honig-Bear. We thank them for laying the foundation for this cookbook.

Rabbi Myra Soifer's guidance was invaluable. Any errors about the holidays are due to our misinterpretations of her scholarly help. Many other people have graciously offered their help. LJ Kutten has generously provided his expertise in formatting the book. Sharrone Blank, Director of Religious Education, inspired the students to create artwork seen throughout the cookbook. Steve Davis graciously allowed us to use one of his photos for our cover.

Thank you to the members and friends who submitted recipes to pass on their traditions. Thank you to the cookbook coordinators: Linda Kutten who typed in the recipes and Adrienne Tropp who wrote the holiday text. Thank you to Nancy Simkin for her great editing, Pam Sloan for the menus, Julie Stage, and many others who contributed time and effort but are not listed above.

Introduction

Recipes from our two previously published cookbooks have been combined and augmented by over a hundred new ones.

Recipes for the holidays as well as other scrumptious foods are in keeping with Jewish dietary laws (kashrut). Milk and meat are not mixed in any recipes and unclean foods (pork, shellfish) are not included. Recipes for Passover make use of the unleavened products that are acceptable for the holiday. Delicious vegetarain recipes are also included.

For your convenience all recipes are labeled as

(D) dairy (milk, butter, cheese)

(M) meat (chicken, poultry, beef)

(P) pareve (fruits, nuts, vegetables, grains, fish, & eggs)

Symbols used in book

▤ Definitions

✔ Tips

✿ Holiday Recipe

⧖ Quick & Easy Meals (see index listing)

✍ Personal Comment

▤ Passover Recipe (see index listing)

We have included a reference section about the Jewish holidays. Spellings and names are anglicized. For instance, instead of Pesach, Passover is used. Dates, origins, greetings, traditional foods, home and synagogue practices, and home activities are provided for the holidays. This is just an overview, a quick reference; for more depth many excellent sources exist. A list of general readings and books with suggested grade levels has been included.

Many traditional "Jewish" recipes are included along with others that we hope will become part of your holiday tradition. Enjoy!

Milestones of Temple Sinai

1962 Temple Sinai was founded by Mary & Jake Garfinkle, Bea & Gene Brown, Judy & Sam Cantor, Fran & Stanley Fielding, and Ruth & Louis Dickens with the aid of Rabbi Joseph Glaser, Northern Pacific Regional Director of UAHC. First High Holy Day Services were held in the Virginia Room of Masonic Temple. A portable Arc was built by Louis Dickens. The San Francisco congregation loaned us a Torah.

1970 February. Ground was broken for construction of Temple Sinai at 3405 Gulling Road in northwest Reno. Louis Dickens offered the 2.96 acre land. Donations of time and materials were made by the congregants. Religious School students planted bushes and trees, celebrating Arbor Day

1970 September. First High Holy days in Temple Sinai at Gulling Road.

1990 August. To overcome our crowded conditions, six classrooms, a library, and two ADA restrooms were added.

1999 The Board of Directors reached a consensus that renovating the existing facility would be cost prohibitive instead we should move to a new facility.

2001 The Building Fund Campaign began. Capital Campaign, General Chairperson Nancy Simkin; Capital Campaign Cabinet Al and Wendy Alderman; Architectural Concept Committee Helene Paris; Property Acquisition Committee Joe Merkin; Architectural Design Wendy Alderman; Finance & Construction Management.

CONTRIBUTORS

Thank you to all who sent in their recipes.

Mary Aaronson
Deborah Achtenberg
Wendy Alderman
Laura Ashkin
Debbie Baer
Emmy Bell
Patricia Blanchard
Beatrice N. Brown
Nancy Daum
Lynne Daus
Steve Davis
Ruth Dickens, of blessed
  memory
Linda Duffié
Patricia Eisenberg
Richard Eisenberg
Carisse Gafni
Gil Gafni
Alan Gertler
Camille Gertler
Selma Goldstein
Martha Gould
Sharon Honig-Bear
Esther Isaac
Ethel Jaffe
Kathryn Karp
Pat Kay
Andi Kaylor
Elizabeth Kempler

Marilyn Kurzman
Linda Kutten
Lori Lacey
Nadine Lipson
Lisa Lowhurst
Marty Matles
Kiersten Mayer
Tinia Merkin
Karen Newman
Rose Orenstein
Helene Paris
Linda Platshon
Debbie Pomeranz
Barbara Pratt
Rabbi Myra Soifer
Zoe Rose
Julia Rubin
Shirley Rutkovitz
Janice Saks
Nancy Simkin
Pam Sloan
George Small
Sharry Springmeyer
Julie Stage
Adelaide Suplin
Adrienne Tropp
Ronnie Varney
Barbara Weinberg

If we missed your name, it was not done intentionally.
We apologize. Thank you.

Table of Contents

SOUPS 79

SALADS 93

BEEF 105

CAKES   229

HOLIDAYS

SHABBAT

A Day of Rest

Date: Shabbat begins every Friday night at sundown and ends at sundown on Saturday.

Purpose: Shabbat provides a day of rest, a day on which work ceases. It is the holiest of all the Jewish celebrations.

Greeting: Shabbat Shalom

Origin: In Genesis, God rests on the seventh day. Exodus 20:8 tells Jews to remember the Sabbath and to keep it holy. In addition, the fourth of the Ten Commandments commands Jews to keep the Sabbath.

Home: Candles are lit, children are blessed, kiddush is said, and the challah is blessed. Shalom Aleichem is sung along with other Shabbat songs. A festival meal is eaten and the Birkat Hamazon is recited. At sundown on Saturday the Havdalah service is performed. A special twisted candle is lid, wine is blessed, and a spice box is passed around.

Synagogue: The service on Friday night begins with the lighting of the candles, welcoming Shabbat (the Kabbalat Shabbat) and the Sabbath Queen. Lecha Dodi is sung to welcome the Sabbath Queen. The formal service begins with the reading of the Barchu, or call to prayer. The Shema proclaims the unity of God. After the Shema, Mi Chamocha is sung. It is the hymn all Israel sang to God after Moses led them from Egypt. Reform congregations may read from Torah on Friday night; other congregations read Torah Saturday morning.

Other: A number of special Shabbats occur during the year. The Rosh Hodesh, before each new moon, is one of these. Others coincide with some of the holidays. At least two candles are lit to acknowledge the pledge to remember and to keep the Sabbath. Candles may be lit for every family member. Often two loaves of challah are placed on the table to symbolize the double portion of manna God provided on the Sabbath. In Jerusalem, in the days of the Temple, the priests would blow the shofar to signal the beginning of the Sabbath.

Food: Foods not normally eaten during the week are savored at the Sabbath dinner. In the Ashkenazi (European) tradition, chicken soup, gefilte fish, and a chicken dish are served. Sephardic (Spanish) traditions feature spicy stuffed meats and rice dishes.

Family: Shabbat is a time for families. Some families spend time playing board games, watching movies, or taking walks. A challah cover, a spice box or tzedakah boxes can be created by younger members of the family.

Readings

It's Challah Time!
by Latifa Berry Kropf, Tod Cohen (Illustrator), Alan Dan Orme, preschool

The Shabbat Box
by Lesley Simpson, Nicole in den Bosch (Illustrator), ages 4-8

The Friday Nights of Nana
by Amy Hest, Claire A. Nivola (Illustrator), ages 4-8

Hanna's Sabbath Dress
by Ora Eitan (Illustrator), Itzhak Schweiger-Dmi'el (Author), ages 4-8

Tales for the Seventh Day: A Collection of Sabbath Stories
by Nina Jaffe, Kelly Stribling Sutherland (Illustrator), ages 4-8

THE JEWISH CALENDAR

The Jewish calendar has 12 months each 29 to 30 days long. It is a lunar-solar calendar with a 19 year cycle. Seven times in the cycle, an additional month (Adar Sheni) is added to assure Passover is celebrated in the Spring as biblically required. The months are:

Nisan	March/April
Iyar	April/May
Sivan	May/June
Tammuz	June/July
Av	July/August
Elul	August/September
Tishri	September/October
Cheshvan	October/November
Kislev	November/December
Tevet	December/January
Shvat	January/February
Adar	February/March
Adar Sheni	*February/March*

SHABBAT

The Torah Scribes

The Hebrew word for scribe is sofer. The scribes of ancient Israel were taught in family-like guilds to become skilled in writing Torah, tefillin, mezuzot and bills of divorce.

To write a Torah, the sofer followed certain procedures and had to be trained in Jewish law. Sofers were paid poorly to prevent them from accruing wealth, therefore encouraging them to continue their work.

The parchment on which the Torah is written must come from the skin of a clean animal, often a sheep. The sofer divides each piece of parchment into three to eight sections, containing forty-two to seventy-two lines.

The Sefer Torah (the scrolls of the Law) must be handwritten using a special indelible black ink prepared from vegetable dyes. The quill is made of the feather of a clean bird, such as a goose or turkey. The tip of the quill is sliced at an angle and has a slit-point to enable the scribe to make either thin or thick strokes.

Before beginning his task, the sofer immerses himself in a mikveh, the ritual bath to purify oneself.

The scribe follows a model copy and uses a special script. Rules are adhered to for decorative flourishes on some of the letters, for spacing certain sections and for requiring which column to begin with the Hebrew letter *vav*. Every word is pronounced before it is written. If an error occurs, the Torah may not be used until the error is corrected. An experienced sofer may take a year to complete the work.

The last few lines of the Torah are finished at a ceremony known as the "Completion of the Sefer Torah."

The scroll is then attached to wooden rollers, called the Tree of Life. The rollers are made of hard wood and have handles of ivory.

Torahs are registered to protect against theft.

ROSH HASHANAH

The Jewish New Year

Date: Rosh Hashanah is the first day of Tishri. In the Gregorian calendar the holiday falls in September or October. Rosh Hashanah never falls on a Sunday, Wednesday, or Friday. For Jews in Israel and Reform synagogues Rosh Hashanah lasts one day. Conservative and orthodox congregations outside Israel celebrate for two days.

Purpose: Rosh Hashanah means the "head of the year." Like the Sabbath it, too, is a time to stop work, renew our spirit and contemplate God.

Greeting: L'Shanah Tovah (Happy new year) or L'Shana Tovah Tikatevu (May you be inscribed for a good year).

Origin: Numbers 29:1 states that on the first day of the seventh month (Tishri), a sacred observance will take place. Furthermore, no work will occur and the shofar will be sounded.

Home: The dinner table is set nicely and flowers often adorn the table. The candles are lit as the sun sets, blessings are said over children, and the Shehehayanu is recited. Then blessings over wine and bread are recited.

Synagogue: On the Saturday night before Rosh Hashanah, a Slichot service is held in which pleas for forgiveness are first recited. On Rosh Hashanah day the Torah is draped in white, as is the Ark. Rabbis wear white. The Avina Malkeinu, the prayer asking for forgiveness and protection, is recited. The Unetaneh Tokef ("On Rosh Hashanah it is written, on Yom Kippur it is sealed. Who shall die and who shall live…") focuses on God's judgment. A service for the sounding of the shofar is also part of the day's ritual.

Other: Tzedakah is one way a person can influence whether his/her name will be written in the "Book of Life." Many synagogues collect food for the needy. Individuals contribute to causes in which they believe. Tashlich (meaning cast off) is a ceremony performed on the afternoon of the first day of Rosh Hashanah. Pockets of lint and breadcrumbs are emptied and tossed into flowing water with the recitation of prayers including one from Micah, "Thou shall toss all your sins into the sea."

Note: The Sabbath between Rosh Hashanah and Yom Kippur is known as Shabbot Shuvah. Memorial candles are lit and penitence is asked.

Food: Three principles apply to selecting food: items should be sweet, round, and abundant. Some examples are challah, apples dipped in honey, honey cakes, raisins, carrot tsimmes, and taiglach (a honey candy). The sweetness symbolize the hope for a sweet year. The roundness symbolizes continuity, the cycle of life, and wholeness. The challah is shaped round, in a circle for this occasion. An abundance of food symbolizes hope for a year of plenty. Salty, bitter or sour foods are avoided. Some people eat fruits they normally do not consume during the rest of the year.

Family: Children can make New Year's cards or cards to celebrate the birth of the world. Tzedakah boxes can be made and decorated.

Readings: Rosh Hashanah and Yom Kippur

On Rosh Hashanah and Yom Kippur (Aladdin Picture Books)
by Melanie W. Hall (Illustrator), Cathy Goldberg Fishman, ages
4-8

The Magic of Kol Nidre : A Story for Yom Kippur
by Bruce H. Siegel, Shelly O. Haas (Illustrator), ages 4-8

Sound the Shofar! : A Story for Rosh Hashanah and Yom Kippur
by Leslie Kimmelman (Author), John Himmelman (Illustrator),
ages 4-8

Gershon's Monster: A Story for the Jewish New Year
by Eric A. Kimmel, Jon J. Muth (Illustrator), Baal Shem Tov,
ages 4-8

When the Chickens Went on Strike
by Erica Silverman, Matthew Trueman (Illustrator), Sholom
Aleichem, grades K-6

ROSH HASHANAH

How Many New Years?

Most consider Rosh Hashanah to be THE Jewish New Year. On Rosh Hashanah we send out New Year's cards and wish each other a "Happy New Year." Rosh Hashanah translates as the "head of the year" when one year advances to the next, i.e., year 5764 becomes 5765. Rosh Hashanah is the beginning of the Jewish religious and economic year as well as the time the new harvest year begins. Rosh Hashanah is the first of Tishri, the seventh month in the Jewish calendar. Sabbatical and Jubilee years begin with Tishri.

Nisan, the first month on the calendar, falls in March or April. Derived from a Babylonian word, Nisan translates as "to start." And it is a start, for dating the reign of kings and the calendar.

The Jewish new years coincide with the beginning of the seasons. The fifteenth of Shevat (usually in February) is the New Year of the Trees. Fruits that ripen prior to the fifteenth belong to the previous year's harvest. Those that are less than one-third their full size on the fifteenth belong to the next year's crop. The house of Shammai proposed the first of Shevat as the new year, but Hillel felt the fifteenth would give people time to prepare.

Elul, usually occurring in August, is the New Year for the Tithing of Cattle. The New Year for Tithing of Cattle and the New Year of the Trees are six months apart.

The Nisan New Year and Rosh Hashanah are followed fourteen days later by harvest festivals: Passover and Succot, respectively. The two festivals are six months apart.

Everyone celebrates numerous new years in a year. Besides the Gregorian calendar new year on January first, we have a fiscal year, a school year, a birthday year, etc.

YOM KIPPUR

The Day of Atonement

Date: Yom Kippur is on the tenth day of Tishri, ten days after Rosh Hashanah.

Purpose: It is a day of fasting and one in which Jews ask for forgiveness for sins committed against God.

Greeting: G'mar Hatimah Tovah (May you be sealed for life for the coming year), Gut Yontif (Yiddish for good holiday) or Hag Sameach (Hebrew for happy holiday). Sometimes: Tzom Kal (May you have an easy fast)

Origin: The Torah tells Jews to mark the tenth day of the seventh month as a day of self-denial. In ancient times the High Priest performed a ceremony to purge the Temple shrine from defilement and one in which a goat (the scapegoat) was sent away with the people's sins to cleanse them. During the time of the Second Temple, the High Priest recited confessions three times.

Home: A meal is eaten before sundown to sustain those who fast. Yahrzeit candles are lit. The blessing over bread is made, but no prayer over wine is recited. After the meal the holiday candles are lit, at which point no more food is eaten and no more work is performed. The Shehehayanu is recited.

Synagogue: Synagogue worship consists of different services. On **The Eve of Yom Kippur** Kol Nidre, the prayer of a people not free to keep their vows, is recited three times. The prayer has a sad, haunting melody. On the **Day of Yom Kippur** four services are held. During the morning service Jews acknowledge they have sinned and recite an alphabetical list of those sins. In the Avinu Malkeanu worshippers ask God to forgive their sins despite their failings. In Reform congregations the Torah service is from Deuteronomy 29:9-14 and 30:11-20 in which the covenant with God is read, and the Haftarah, from Isaiah 58:1-14, tells the proper way to fast. During the afternoon service parts of Leviticus are read; the Haftarah portion is from the Book of Jonah. A Yizkor memorial service takes place during the day. The Ne'ilah (the closing of the gates, originally the Temple gates but now meant as the gates of heaven) service concludes the day's prayers. The Shofar is blown and Yom Kippur comes to an end.

Other: Leather, make-up, and perfume are not worn. Sex is prohibited. The day is for tending to spiritual needs. White is worn, for some a Kittel (white robe). Tzedakah is given to the poor. An interesting custom: on the day before Yom Kippur a man took a rooster and a woman a hen and swung them three times in a prescribed manner to cast out sins. The meat went to the poor as a form of Tzedakah.

Food: None. This is fast day. **Before the fast** people eat foods high in carbohydrates and drink plenty of water but avoid salty or well-seasoned foods. The **break-the-fast** often consists of light dairy: lox, bagels, herring, fish, sweets, kugels, orange juice and coffee.

Family: This is a good time of year for families to discuss ways to treat members better. Tzedakah projects should be undertaken, especially giving food to the poor.

SUKKOT

The Feast of the Booths or Time of Our Rejoicing

Date: Sukkot, a seven day holiday for Jews in Israel and Reform Jews, occurs four days after Yom Kipper. Traditional Jews celebrate for eight days. It begins on the fifteenth day of Tishri, when the moon is full and the rainy season is about to begin.

Purpose: Sukkot is one of three pilgrimage festivals and a time to celebrate the bounty of the harvest. It also commemorates the period during which the Jewish people wandered in the desert and lived in temporary structures, called sukkot.

Greeting: Hag Sameach (Happy holiday)

Origin: Deuteronomy 16:13 and Leviticus 23:42-43 command Jews to celebrate the harvest and live in booths for seven days. Numbers 29:12-34 describes the pattern of sacrifice during the holiday. Many ancient people celebrated a successful harvest.

Home: At sunset candles are lit. The blessing over wine is recited in the sukkah and then the Shehehayanu and a blessing acknowledging the privilege of celebrating Sukkot are recited. Next, a round challah is dipped in honey and blessed. Meals are eaten in the sukkah. After the meal Birkat Hamazon, a prayer of thanksgiving, is said.

SUKKOT

Synagogue: Torah portions associated with the holiday are read, and The Hallel (praise) is recited. The etrog and lulav are waved in a prescribed manner during services. The etrog, a yellow citrus fruit like a lemon but has a pittom, a small blossom at the end, is held in the left hand. The lulav consists of the lulav (a palm branch), the hadas (myrtle branch) and arava (willow branch) that are all held together in the right hand.

Other: Solomon consecrated the Second Temple on Sukkot. As a pilgrimage holiday people traditionally flocked to Jerusalem with gifts of animals, grains, fruit, etc. and lived in harvester huts (like the sukkah). It was a joyous time in which torches were lit and a water dance performed. The American Thanksgiving holiday traces its roots to Sukkot and the Biblical command to celebrate the harvest.

Food: Foods associated with the fall harvest are eaten as are foods such as stuffed cabbage, kreplach and strudel since stuffed foods symbolize plenty/abundance.

Family: Build a sukkah; kits are available. The sukkah is closely associated with the holiday. The building of it follows certain requirements. It should be rectangular, be large enough for at least one person to stand up, have at least three temporary walls, be strong enough to withstand high winds, and provide shade but allow for the stars to shine through. Dangling from the roof are apples, oranges, grapes, onions, corn, greenery, etc. Hand-made decorations adorn the sukkah, as well. Meals are eaten within and some even sleep there. It is a tradition to invite in ancestors such as Abraham or Sarah and other guests. Children can draw pictures to place inside or perhaps make their own miniature sukkah from a shoebox. Etrog boxes can be made and decorated.

Readings

The Sukkah That I Built
by Rochel Groner Vorst, Elizabeth Victor-Elsby (Illustrator),
baby and preschool

All About Sukkot
by Judyth Saypol Groner, Madeline Wikler, Kinny Kreiswirth
(illustrator), ages 4-8

Harvest Festivals

Civilizations that depend on agriculture offer thanks for a bountiful season. The Israelite civilization was one of them. They had three harvest seasons and accompanying celebrations:

❦Barley was harvested in April or May. This coincides with Passover.

❦Wheat ripened about seven weeks later which is Shavuot.

❦Fruits ripened in September or October and Sukkot is celebrated.

After each harvest a pilgrimage was made to the Temple in Jerusalem to offer thanks. Burnt offerings were made and the poor were fed.

The harvest seasons began with Passover and ended with Sukkot. Sukkot is referred to as "The Festival" and involved the greatest celebration perhaps because it ended the year's cycle. Sukkot is also known as the Feast of the Tabernacles and Shavuot as Penticost, a Greek word meaning fifty.

SUKKOT

Sukkot and Ecclesiastes

Ecclesiastes, one of the five megillot, is reputed to be the work of Solomon in his old age, a time when he felt the gloom of approaching death. The Hebrew title for the work is Kohelet, meaning preacher. Ecclesiastes is the Greek translation of Kohelet. The writer identifies himself as the son of David and the King of Israel. Scholars, though, have doubts of Solomon's authorship because of the anachronistic use of language.

Most of Ecclesiastes reads like a prose essay, and words from Ecclesiastes are familiar to all of us: "To everything there is a season," and "Vanity of vanity, all is vanity." Much of Ecclesiastes conveys the sober message about how life lacks meaning and purpose. Jewish sages have pointed out that without Torah life has no purpose.

So why is this megillah read on the Shabbat during Sukkot? Scholars have offered several explanations. Since Ecclesiastes tells that life is transient, like the sukkah we inhabit during this holiday, it is an appropriate reading for the holiday. Some scholars believe we read the words of Kohelet because the sages feared the Sukkot celebration would get out of hand and the reading provides a balance. Others point to the words "To everything there is a season and a time to every purpose under heaven… a time to plant and a time to pluck what is planted… a time to weep and a time to laugh" as an appropriate message for a holiday that follows closely upon the High Holidays and is a celebration of the fruit harvest.

SIMCHAT TORAH

Rejoicing of the Law

Date: Simchat Torah follows Sukkot and occurs on the twenty-third of Tishrei.

Purpose: Simchat Torah is a joyous holiday, celebrating the completion of Deuteronomy (the last of the Five Books of Moses) and the immediate beginning of Genesis. The holiday honors the importance of Torah in the life of the Jewish people.

Greeting: Hag Sameach (Happy holiday!)

Origin: The holiday was first celebrated when the Jewish people were in exile in Babylonia. It reaffirms the dedication of the exiled people to Torah. Because Deuteronomy tells of Moses' death, and is immediately followed by Genesis telling of creation, a message of hope and rebirth fills the holiday spirit.

Home: Candles are lit at sundown, children are blessed, the blessing over wine is recited and the challah is, for the last time during the holiday season, dipped in honey. The Birkat Hamazon is sung. A festival meal is served.

Synagogue: A joyous and boisterous celebration occurs at synagogue. All Torahs are taken from the Ark, and everyone dances with the scrolls. The direction of the dance may change and the music speeds up. A procession is made seven times around the sanctuary. Some congregations head outside to celebrate. The Torah is traditionally passed from person to person. Children carry Israeli flags with apples and sometimes candles affixed to the top. A synagogue member, perhaps the oldest or a leader, benefactor or teacher of the congregation, is given an aliyah. In some congregations, a tallit is held above the heads of children (those under bar/bat mitzvah age), and they, as a group, are given a special aliyah known as Kol Hanearim or the voice of all the children. The Haftarah portion tells of Joshua, the anointed leader after Moses, crossing the Jordan into Israel. In many synagogues a consecration ceremony is held, honoring the youngest members as they begin their Jewish studies.

Food: None specifically.

Family: Make Israeli flags. Decorate a cake in the shape of the Torah.

♪ The Israeli Flag ♪

The Israeli flag was designed in 1897 by the First Zionist Congress.

It is white (the color of newness and purity), and has two blue stripes (the color of heaven) like the stripes of the tallit. The tallit is the prayer shawl, which symbolizes the transmission of Jewish tradition.

In its center is the Star of David.

Later the dark sky blue was lightened for better visibility.

HANUKKAH
Rededication of the Temple

Date: Hanukkah begins on the twenty-fifth of Kislev and lasts eight days. In the Gregorian calendar it may fall between the end of November and the end of December.

Purpose: Hanukkah celebrates the rededication of the Temple.

Greeting: Hag Sameach (Happy holiday)

Origin: King Antiochus Epiphanes outlawed circumcision, eating Kosher foods and observing the Sabbath to force the Jewish people to worship Greek gods. A rebellion by Mattathias and his five sons, known as the Maccabees, began when a Jewish man sacrificed a pig on the Temple altar on orders of the king. A successful guerrilla-like war ensued under the leadership of Mattathias's son Judah. After their victory, the Maccabees restored the Temple and rebuilt the desecrated altar. It was rededicated on the twenty-fifth of Kislev, probably in 165 BCE According to legend there had been only enough oil to burn in the Temple's menorah for one day, but the oil lasted for eight. Another prominent belief given for the eight-day celebration is because Jews had been unable to celebrate the eight-day Sukkot holiday due to the restrictive Greek laws, the rededication became a belated Sukkot celebration.

Home: A menorah, or, more properly, hanukiyah is lit for eight nights. The shamash or servant candle is separated from the other candles and is used to light the others. The hanukiyah should be seen from the street. The first candle is placed on the far right as you face the hanukiyah. Candles are added from the left and lit from left to right. It is traditional for everyone to have a hanukiyah, light it, and say the prayers. On the first night the Shehehayanu is recited. On Friday night the Sabbath candles are lit last.

Synagogue: The section from The Book of Numbers about the rededication of the Temple is read. The Haftarah is the portion from Zachariah 2:14 - 4:7 with the words, "Not by might, not by power, but by spirit alone shall all people live in peace."

Food: Foods cooked in oil are eaten. Latkes of all types from potato to cauliflower to cheese are popular. In Israel sufganiot (jelly donuts) are eaten. Cookies in the shapes of dreidels, Stars of David, and menorahs are fun to bake and decorate.

Family: According to legend, Jews continued to study together in spite of the King's ban on Judaism. To fool soldiers, books were quickly squirreled away and the dreidel spun in the gathering. To play dreidel, everyone throws something – beans, pennies, candy – into the middle of the table. A person who spins *nun* gets nothing; *gimmel*, takes all; *hay* receives half; *shin* antes up more for the pot. The initial letters of the phrase *nun, gimmel, hay, shin* translate as "A great miracle happened there." Ma-oz Tzur or Rock of Ages is sung. Gifts are given, often for each night of the holiday. It is traditional in the United States to give gelt, money. Craft a menorah constructed from wood or fashioned from clay. For the candles, use bottle caps or nuts. Make decorations to hang: banners, dreidel shapes, a Star of David, etc. Have a party exchanging inexpensive grab bag gifts. Besides playing dreidel, kids can pin the sword on the Maccabee or the shamash on a Hanukiyah.

HANUKKAH

Readings

The Hanukkah Mice
by Ronne Randall, Maggie Kneen (Illustrator), ages 2-6

The Chanukkah Guest
by Eric A. Kimmel, Giora Carmi (Illustrator), ages 4-8

A Hanukkah Treasury
by Eric A. Kimmel (Editor), Emily Lisker (Illustrator), ages 4-8

It's a Miracle! : A Hanukkah Storybook
by Stephanie Spinner (Author), Jill McElmurry (Illustrator), ages 4-8

Lots of Latkes: A Hanukkah Story
by Sandy Lanton, Vicki Jo Redenbaugh (Illustrator), ages 4-8

One Candle
by Eve Bunting (Author), K. Wendy Popp (Illustrator), ages 4-8

The Peddler's Gift
by Maxine Rose Schur, Kimberly Bulcken Root, Diane Arico (Editor), ages 4-8

When Mindy Saved Hanukkah
by Eric A. Kimmel, Barbara McClintock (Illustrator), ages 4-8

Hershel and the Hanukkah Goblins
by Eric Kimmel (Author) age 4-8

Alexandra's Scroll: The Story of the First Hanukkah
by Miriam Chaikin, Stephen Fieser (Illustrator), ages 9-12

The Magic Menorah : A Modern Chanukah Tale
by Jane Breskin Zalben (Author), Donna Diamond (Illustrator), ages 9-12

The Jar of Fools: Eight Hanukkah Stories from Chelm
by Eric A. Kimmel, Mordicai Gerstein (Illustrator), ages 9-12

HANUKKAH

The Stone Lamp: Eight Stories Of Hanukkah Through History
by Karen Hesse, Brian Pinkney, ages 9-12

The Power of Light: Eight Stories for Hanukkah
by Isaac Bashevis Singer (Author), Irene Lieblich (Illustrator),
all ages

The Maccabean Period

The rededication of the Temple in 165 BCE marks the beginning of the Maccabean period, but perhaps the period should more rightfully be called the Hasmonean period.

It began when Mattathias, a priest and member of the Hasmonean family, refused to obey Antiochus IV orders to abandon Jewish practices. Antiochus defiled the Temple. Mattathias and his five sons rose in opposition. Upon Mattathias's death Judas (or Judah) took lead with guerilla type attacks on the Syrians. Maccabees, meaning hammer, was first applied to Juda because of the hammer blows he struck against his enemies. Judas's death in 160 BCE passed the hammer to his brothers Jonathan then to Simon who continued fighting until independence was won. Peace lasted until 134 BCE. Simon was murdered by his son-in-law. Simon's son, John Hyrcanus, emerged as the high priest/king, reigning a period of peace and prosperity until his death in about105 BCE. Then unrest redeveloped. John's son Aristobulus reigned for a year until his death. He was succeeded by his brother Alexander Jannaeus who governed harshly. His widow Salome Alexandra followed and ruled wisely for eight years but she favored the Pharisees. After her death in 69 BCE, civil war broke out between the Pharisees and the Sadducees. Pompey was called upon to quell the disquiet. He ultimately put an end to Maccabean rule and the freedom Mattathias had sought.

Tu B'Shevat

New Year of the Trees

Date: Tu B'Shevat is on the fifteenth of Shevat, falling either in January or February.

Purpose: This agricultural holiday celebrates the earth and its produce. It occurs after the heavy rains have fallen in Israel. Jews are also commanded to care for the earth.

Origin: The fifteenth of Shevat was the ancient equivalent of April 15th. It was the day after all fruit was harvested and a count could be made of the amount. People were assessed one-tenth, a tithe, which they brought to the Temple. Genesis 1:11-13 is read. This portion of the Torah emphasizes the need to care for the land.

Home: Individuals purchase trees for Israel. Candles are not lit. People eat the seven types of plants mentioned in Deuteronomy 8:8 - wheat, barley, grapes, figs, pomegranate, olives and dates. A Tu B'Shevat seder may be held. Although not fixed by custom, the seder consists of four cups of wine and special fruits. The first course is fruits that are totally consumed such as grapes; the second course is fruits with inedible pits (olives, plums); the last course is hard shelled nuts (coconuts). These courses symbolize mystical levels of creation. Wine is drunk between each of the three courses. Each cup of wine varies by color to represent the changing seasons. The first is white wine, then pink (a mixture of white and red), deep rose and finally red (with just a drop of white wine).

Synagogue: During synagogue worship Genesis 1:11-13, Leviticus 19:23-25 and Psalm 65:10-12 are read. These selections emphasize the need for people to care for the earth and contemplate their relationship to it.

Food: Eat the plants mentioned above as well as more modern fruits like oranges, avocados, bananas, kiwi and carob (bokar in Yiddish).

Family: On Tu B'Shevat in 1949, just after Israeli independence, thousands gathered to plant life-giving trees in a forest. The forest known as the "Forest of Martyrs," commemorates the six million Jews who died in concentration camps. It is traditional in the United States to donate money to plant trees in Israel. Giving tzedakah to the needy and contributing to environmental causes are two rites for this holiday. Make recycling bins. Plant herbs.

Readings

Solomon and the Trees
by Matt Biers-Ariel, Esti Silverberg-Kiss (Illustrator), ages 4-8

The Giving Tree
by Shel Silverstein, ages 4-8

Ecology & the Jewish Spirit: Where Nature and the Sacred Meet
by Ellen Bernstein (Editor), adult

Torah of the Earth: Exploring 4,000 Years of Ecology in Jewish Thought
by Arthur Waskow (Editor), adult

PURIM

Feast of Lots

Date: Purim falls on the fourteenth of Adar, usually in February or March.

Purpose: This joyous holiday celebrates the victory and deliverance of the Jewish people from their enemies.

Origin: Queen Esther's story is told in the Book of Esther. Esther is a Jewish woman who becomes queen and is in a position to save the Jewish people from Haman. Haman, an evil advisor to King Ahashuerus, sought the death of all Jews in Persia because they would not bow before him nor follow Persian customs. Unwittingly, the king agreed to their death. Haman drew lots (pur) to determine what day the Jewish people would die. Mordechai, Esther's uncle, alerted Esther to the plot. She told King Ahashuerus who ordered Haman's death. Centuries earlier, Amalek, one of Haman's forefathers, had led the Amalekites against the Israelites as they fled Egypt.

Home: Candles are not lit on Purim. Instead it is traditional to give simple gifts to friends (known as mishloah manot) and food to the poor. Some gifts should be given in person. Gifts to friends are usually baked goods or homemade craft items.

Synagogue: The Megillah, the Book of Esther, is read at synagogue. There are five megillot. When Jews refer to The

Megillah, they mean the Book of Esther. During services whenever Haman's name is mentioned, congregants boo, scream, bang, or shake their groggers (noisemakers) to blot out his name. When Esther or Mordechai's names are mentioned, worshippers instead call out "Yea!" To add to the festivities, costumes are worn to synagogue. The Haftarah portion on the Sabbath prior to Purim tells of King Saul's inability to destroy the Amalekites.

Food: Hamantaschen, a three-sided pastry that resembles Haman's hat, is eaten on this holiday. Some also eat kreplach.

Family: Bake hamantaschen. Also make food or craft gifts to give others. Make groggers by placing beans in a can or between two paper plates and be sure to seal the can or plates well. Making any type of costume from that of clowns to queens is part of the holiday fun.

Readings

Queen Esther The Morning Star
by Mordicai Gerstein (Illustrator), ages 2-5

Queen Esther Saves Her People
by Rita Golden Gelman, Frane Lessac (Illustrator), Fran E. Lessac (Illustrator), ages 4-8

Every Person's Guide to Purim
by Ronald H. Isaacs, adult

PASSOVER

A Celebration of Freedom

Date: Passover begins on the fifteenth of Nisan (March or April). Reform Jews and Israelis celebrate the holiday for seven days; others for eight.

Purpose: At Passover, the story of the Israelites' bondage and their escape from Egypt is told. It is incumbent upon all Jews to tell this story to their children. Pesach is a celebration of freedom.

Origin: Passover is the story of the Exodus from Egypt.

Home: A seder (meaning order) is a ritual meal in which participants read from the Haggadah, which tells why we celebrate Passover, how to conduct a seder, and what various symbols mean. For the seder table a plate with karpas (a leafy green vegetable), maror (bitter herbs), a roasted shank bone, Charoset (a mixture of fruit, nuts, wine and spices), and a roasted egg is laid out. Three matzot are placed on the table as well as salt water for dipping. A wine cup for Elijah is also placed on the table. More recently, a wine cup for Miriam has also been set out. The format of the seder was essentially finalized in the eleventh century.

Synagogue: Passover worship is similar to worship on Sukkot and Shavuot, the other two pilgrimage festivals. On the Sabbath during Passover many congregations read the Song of Songs before the Torah portion. The Torah portions are from Exodus 33:12 – 34:26 and Numbers 28:19-25. The Exodus portion tells of Moses seeking out God, and Numbers tells of the burnt offerings for the holiday. The Haftarah portion is Ezekiel 37 about Ezekiel's experience in the valley of dry bones. These portions connect past redemption to future redemption.

Other: The first and last days of Passover are holy days; the intermediate days are half-holidays.

Food: Matzo and unleavened foods are eaten during Passover. Matzo balls and chicken soup are traditional. Various Charoset recipes are popular.

Family: Make and decorate matzo covers from napkins. Search and get rid of hametz, leavened goods. Make donations, especially of food, to the poor.

Readings

The Matzah That Papa Brought Home
by Fran Manushkin, Ned Bittinger (Illustrator), baby to preschool

The Matzah Man: A Passover Story
by Naomi Howland, preschool to second grade

Matzo Ball Moon
by Leslea Newman, Elaine Greenstein (Illustrator), ages 4-8

Miriam's Cup: A Passover Story
by Fran Manushkin, Bob Dacey (Illustrator) ages 4-8

Pearl's Passover: A Family Celebration Through Stories, Recipes, Crafts, and Songs
by Jane Breskin Zalben (Illustrator), ages 4-8

PASSOVER

Angels Sweep the Desert Floor: Biblical Stories about Moses in the Wilderness
by Miriam Chaiken, grades 4-7

The Haggadah

Haggadah is a Hebrew word which essentially means narrate, narrating the Exodus from Egypt. The first story of the Exodus was made over two thousand years ago. Originally, the Exodus was part of the prayer book, but as songs, prayers, hymns, and selections from Mishna were added the need for a separate written Haggadah developed. In the 1500's about 25 different types of Haggadah existed. The number has proliferated now to over three thousand versions. They range from traditional ones to those adapted to women's rights, gays and lesbians, vegetarians, etc. Many construct their own Haggadahs, using the best parts from others.

The format we follow today was formalized about 1800 years ago. Dayenu is one of the oldest selections. Chad Gadya was originally in Aramaic and became part of the Seder around 1200. Even the four questions evolved in content over the years. Many of the customs in the Haggadah came to us from the Greeks and Romans.

Since this is a story to tell children, Haggadahs may have originally been illustrated for their enjoyment. A Haggadah from southern Germany of the 1300's is known as the Bird's Head Haggadah. Most of the humans illustrated have birds' heads, including beaks. Some were given short pointed animal ears. These artistic depictions probably followed the early tradition of not creating graven human images.

PASSOVER

Ashkenazic and Sephardic Passover Customs

Passover celebrations vary according to culture. Sephardic (meaning Spanish) is applied to Jews from Spain, Portugal and northern Africa; while Ashkenazic (meaning German) refers to Jews who settled in central and eastern Europe.

Ashkenazic Jews will eat potatoes but avoid the lamb, rice, beans, peas, green beans, corn, sunflower and caraway seeds that Sephardim eat. Ashkenazim will use matzo meal while Sephardim tend to crush their own matzo for use.

The seder tables vary. Only the Ashkenazim set a cup for Elijah. The Ashkenazic seder plate has karpas (often parsley), maror (often horseradish), roasted shank bone, Charoset, and a roasted egg. Salt water is placed in separate bowls. Charoset is made of sweet wine, nuts, apples, honey, and cinnamon. The Sephardic seder plate also includes the matzo along with the karpas (celery leaves, parsley or boiled potato) and maror (endive, romaine, or escarole). Dates or figs predominate in the Charoset. Each item on the plate has a kabbalistic meaning for Sephardim.

Ashkenazic Jews hide the middle matzo and ransom it back for dessert. Sephardic Jews tie up the afikomon in a napkin for one of their children to sling it over his or her shoulder and re-enact the exodus from Egypt while the seder leader asks the three questions about the journey.

Sephardic Jews ask in unison the four questions in this order: why do we dip twice, why do we eat matzo, why do we eat maror and why do we eat reclining. Ashkenazic Jews change the order and ask the youngest only, first about the matzo, then about the maror, dipping twice, and finally reclining.

YOM HASHOAH

Holocaust Memorial Day

Date: After much debate by the Israeli Knesset, the twenty-seventh of Nisan was selected as Yom HaShoah. It is the twelfth day of the Omer and occurs five days after Passover.

Purpose: This day is a remembrance of those Jews who lost their lives during the Holocaust. Not only is it a day to recall those murdered by the Nazis, but also to offer hope that the world will never again experience a Holocaust.

Origin: On April 12, 1951 the Knesset voted to make the twenty-seventh of Nisan a day of remembrance. In 1959, it became a public holiday, and in 1961 the Knesset voted to close all public entertainments on Yom HaShoah. "Shoah" is the Hebrew equivalent of the English word "Holocaust." It literally means a whirlwind, a conflagration.

Home: Since this is a recent holy day, Yom HaShaoah practices are still developing. Home services may include the lighting of one or six (for the six million Jews murdered during the Holocaust) candles. People on the street should be able to view the candles. Yellow candles are becoming more common. Family members should share stories about the Holocaust, "Lest we forget."

Synagogue: Synagogue worship is also new and developing.

YOM HASHOAH

Lighting candles and listening to survivors' accounts are common practice. In Reform temples the ma'ariv service is read. Kiddish is said.

Other: Community remembrances are also becoming more common. These may include lighting of memorial candles and reading of the names of those killed. Holocaust survivors are asked to speak. Prayers, poems, and songs are shared.

Family: Write poems about the Holocaust, view movies such as *Schindler's List*, or read age appropriate books together.

Readings

The Number on My Grandfather's Arm
by David A. Adler, Rose Eichenbaum (Photographer), grades 1-4

The Devil's Arithmetic
by Jane Yolen, ages 9-12

Number the Stars
by Lois Lowrey, ages 9-12

Diary of a Young Girl
by Anne Frank, grades 8 and above

Night
by Elie Wiesel, teen to adult

The Holocaust: A History of the Jews of Europe During the Second World War
by Martin Gilbert, teen to adult

Maus : A Survivor's Tale : My Father Bleeds History/Here My Troubles Began/Boxed
by Art Spiegelman, teen to adult

The Columbia Guide to the Holocaust
by Donald L. Niewyk, Francis R. Nicosia, adult

YOM HASHOAH

LAG BaOMER

Thirty-Third Day of Omer

Date: Usually in April, Lag BaOmer falls on the eighteenth of Iyar, thirty-four days after Passover begins.

Purpose: Lag BaOmer is a feast day, a respite from the semi-mourning of the Omer period.

Origin: Lag BaOmer actually refers to the thirty-third (in Hebrew, thirty is *lamed* and three is *gimel*) day in the count of the Omer. The Omer was an offering of barley made on the second day of Pesach at the Temple. The Omer is a count that begins on that day and continues until the fiftieth day, Shavuot. According to tradition 24,000 of Rabbi Akiva's students perished during a plague because they had not shown respect toward one another; however, none died on the thirty-third day. It is also the day Rabbi Shimon bar Yochai died. He is reputed to be the author of the mystical work the Zohar (*The Shining Light*), the basis of Kabbalah. Because his work was completed before he died, the day is one of celebration.

Family: Feasts, picnics, outings are planned for this day. In Israel people visit Yochai's grave at Meron. Bonfires are lit to commemorate the fire that had burned around his house but still allowed his closest pupils to enter. Shooting contests with bows and rubber-tipped arrows take place. According to legend, Rabbi Akiva's students would steal to the forest to study Torah but carried bows and arrows to appear like hunters.

Judaism Timeline To The Diaspora

Sources disagree on dates.
Many of the given dates are approximate.

BCE
1800-1300   Period of the Patriarchs
1300   Moses leads Hebrews out of Egypt
1270   Conquest of Promised Land
1000-925   Time of David and Solomon, First Temple
            Built, The Torah is assembled, Psalms written
925   Israel splits into Judah and Israel (Samaria)
925-587   The writings of the Prophets
586   Jews taken into exile by Babylonian King
            Nebuchadnezzar II
539   Persians capture Babylon; some Jews return to
            Israel
355   Esther and Purim
300   The Hebrew Bible is assembled,
            Second Temple is built
168-164   Maccabee rebellion, rededication of the
            Temple, Judea was free
30   Romans in Galilee, Samaria and
            Judea, Time of Hillel and Shammai
CE
70   Romans destroy Jerusalem and Temple
132-135   Time of Akiva, bar Yohai and bar Kochba

BEGINNING OF THE DIASPORA
219   Mishna written by Rabbi Judah the Prince
            (Yehudah Ha-Nasi)

SHAVUOT

Giving of the Torah

Date: Shavuot is fifty days after the first day or seven weeks after the second day of Passover. It is on the sixth and seventh days of Sivan in traditional congregations that celebrate it as a two-day holiday. This will fall in late April or early May.

Purpose: Shavuot celebrates the day the Torah was received. It has come to affirm Jewish study and education. In many congregations confirmation is held on this day.

Origin: The word shavuot means weeks, to mark the fact that the holiday is seven weeks after Pesach. Originally, it was a harvest holiday (one of three throughout the year) to celebrate the end of the barley harvest and the beginning of the wheat harvest, as well as the ripening of the first fruits. The two loaves of wheat bread that were brought to the Temple symbolized what people have made from what God has provided. The rabbis calculated that the Torah was given to Moses at this time, and the celebration evolved into one emphasizing the giving of Torah.

Home: Candles are lit, the prayer over wine is recited, and challah is blessed. Dairy meals are popular. Decorate with flowers or plants.

Synagogue: Yizkor is recited and the Book of Ruth is read. The

Torah portion tells of the giving of the Torah and the Ten Commandments. The Haftarah comes from Ezekiel. Many congregations now have a confirmation ceremony in which sixteen-year olds rededicate themselves to Judaism. The all-night study session common in some congregations concludes with an outdoor sunrise service.

Other: In Europe Jews would introduce their young children to the Torah and provide honey and sweets.

Food: Numerous reasons are given for why dairy is associated with the holiday, but none is officially recognized. Blintzes and cheesecake are especially popular, and some make extra long challots to commemorate the two loaves of wheat bread.

Ruth and Shavuot

Ruth is one of the five megillot and is read at Shavuot. The Book of Ruth is a more obvious choice for Shavuot than Ecclesiastes is for Sukkot.

Ruth, a widow, remains faithful to her mother-in-law and accompanies her back to Judah. In order to have food, Naomi tells Ruth to follow the reapers. She gleans the barley leavings from the field of Boaz, a relative of her deceased husband. Laws permitted the poor to glean from the fields. Eventually Ruth marries Boaz and they have offspring. One of her descendents is David.

The Book of Ruth has three associations with Shavuot. Like Shavuot The Book of Ruth takes place in the spring as barley is harvested. According to tradition David was born and died on Shavuot. Shavuot is also the time of the giving of the Torah. By converting to Judaism, Ruth accepts Torah.

Yom HaAtzmaut

Israel Independence Day

Date: Yom HaAtzmaut is the fifth of Iyar, the twentieth day in the count of the Omer, the date in the Hebrew calendar that Israel gained its independence. On the Gregorian calendar that date was May14,1948.

Purpose: The day celebrates the date Israel achieved its independence. The day preceding is Yom Hazikaron or Day of Remembrance for those who lost their lives in helping to establish or defend Israel.

Origin: In November 1947, The United Nations voted to partition Palestine, an area controlled by the British, and establish the State of Israel. At 4 p.m. on May 14,1948, the British lowered their flag and the flag of Israel was raised. The First Zionist Conference had designed the flag in 1897. On May 14, David Ben Gurion read the Proclamation of Independence over the radio. Unfortunately, five Arab nations attacked that same day. After a prolonged battle, Israel ended up with more land than the original proclamation had provided

Israel: In Israel on Yom Hazikaron, a siren sounds at 8 p.m. and at 11 a.m. for everyone to observe two minutes of silence in honor of those who gave their lives for Israel. Then at sunset pandemonium breaks out as people celebrate independence. Fireworks, parades, songs and dances liven the celebration.

Food: No foods are associated with the holiday, but eating Israeli foods such as falafel would add to the holiday spirit.

Family: Make an Israeli flag. Listen and sing along to Hatikvah. Dance the hora or other Israeli dances.

YOM HAATZMAUT

The Declaration of the Establishment of the State of Israel May 14, 1948

David Ben Gurion read over the radio:

"The Land of Israel was the birthplace of the Jewish people. Here the spiritual, religious and national identity was formed. Here they achieved independence and created a culture of national and universal significance. Here they wrote and gave the Bible to the world...

"Exiled from Palestine, the Jewish people remained faithful to it in all the countries of the dispersion, never ceasing to pray and hope for their return and restoration of their national freedom.

"Accordingly we, the members of the National Council met together in solemn assembly today and by virtue of the natural and historic right of the Jewish people and with the support of the resolution of the General of the United Nations, hereby proclaim the establishment of the Jewish state in Palestine to be called Israel...

"We offer peace and amity to all neighboring states and their peoples and invite them to cooperate with the independent Jewish nation for the common good of all...

"With trust in the Rock of Israel, we set our hands to this declaration at this session of the Provisional State Council in the city of Tel Aviv on Sabbath Eve, 5th Iyar 5708, 14th day of May 1948."

TISHA B'AV

A Day of Mourning

Date: Tisha B'Av is on the ninth day of Av (late July or early August).

Purpose: This solemn holiday is a day of fasting and sorrow, a time for self-reflection.

Origin: Although hundreds of years apart, the ninth of Av represents the date both the First and Second Temples were destroyed. The Babylonians destroyed the First Temple in 586 BCE, and the Romans destroyed the Second Temple in 70 CE. The loss of the Temples reflects the loss of Jewish independence and raises a profound theological question on whether God has left the Jewish people.

Home: Eating, drinking, bathing, shaving, perfume, leather and sex are prohibited at this time.

Synagogue: Lamentations and Job are read, but toward the end of worship services hymns of hope replace the hymns of sadness. Haftarah portions may include readings from Deuteronomy 4:25-40, Jeremiah 8:13-9:23, Exodus 32:11-14 and 34:1-10 and Isaiah 55:6-56:8. The Ark is draped in black and the light from burning candles barely illuminates the sanctuary. People may sit on the floor or on low benches. The mourner's Kaddish is recited and perhaps the Ani Ma'amin, about the coming of the Messiah.

Other: Not only is the ninth of Av associated with the destruction of both Temples, but other calamitous events are associated with that date: 1190, the population of York, England was massacred; 1290, Edward I banished all Jews; 1492, the expulsion of Jews from Spain; 1942, Nazis began the deportation of Jews from Warsaw. Music, weddings, haircuts and new clothing are banned during a three-week period prior to and including Tisha B'Av. If in Israel visit the Wailing Wall, hike around the walls of the Old City, or visit archeological diggings where the approaches to the Temple can be seen.

Food: None. This is a fast day. Before the fast, people may eat hard round rolls, bagels, eggs, bread sprinkled with ashes, lentils, uncooked fruits or vegetables – foods associated with mourning.

The Temples

First Temple, built by Solomon, 180 feet long, 90 feet wide, and 50 feet high, used cedar imported from Tyre and huge quarried stones. Inside, the Holy of Holies contained the Ten Commandments. The High Priest entered the room once a year, only on Yom Kippur. The Babylonians destroyed the Temple about 400 years after it was built.

Second Temple, built on the site of the first, was made of white marble covered in gold. Inside were a menorah made by Moses and a golden table for the twelve loaves of bread for the Sabbath. In the Holy of Holies a block of marble replaced the Ark of the Covenant. Herod commanded 1000 priests, trained as masons, to rebuild the Temple because only priests were allowed upon the sacred ground. Today the Temple platform, about 35 acres, and part of the Western Wall are all that survive.

TERMS

(As Used in Text)

Akiva, Rabbi – respected leader killed in 135 CE fighting against the Romans

Agriculture holidays – Sukkot, Shavuot, and Passover

Aliyah – literally Hebrew for "going up," the honor of being called up to Torah.

Amidah – a long silent prayer

Ark – closed cabinet where Torah scrolls are kept

Barchu – a formal call to prayer

Birkat Hamazon – prayers that offer thanks for food

Challah – loaf of braided egg bread used on the Sabbath and for festivals

Confirmation – similar to a graduation from religious school

Dreidel – a spinning top with the Hebrew letters *nun, gimel, hay,* and *shin*

Elijah – Biblical prophet who will announce the coming of the Messiah

Haftarah – the reading from the Prophets that concludes the Torah reading

Haggadah – book containing Exodus and the ritual of the Seder

Hanukiyah – the nine-branched Hanukkah menorah,

Havdalah – the service that concludes the Sabbath

Holocaust – the genocide of European Jews during World War II by the Nazis

Kabbalah – mystical Jewish teachings

Kaddish – a hymn of praise to God and a prayer for the dead

Kiddush – blessing over wine or a light meal after the wine

Knesset – an assembly, specifically the Israeli parliament

Ma'ariv – evening prayer service

Megillot – five scrolls, when capitalized the Book of Esther

Menorah – a seven-branched candelabrum

Miriam – a prophetess and sister of Moses

Moses – great prophet who brought the Jewish people out of slavery from Egypt, lead them in the desert for forty years, taught them to follow the laws of the Torah

Omer – forty-nine days between Passover and Shavuot, originally a time when the grain ripened in the fields

Pilgrimage Festivals – Passover, Sukkot and Shavuot

TERMS

Rosh Hodesh – the first day of the new month, the time when the new moon appears

Seder – order, prayers and rituals for home celebration

Shema – prayer proclaiming Jewish belief in one God

Shalom – peace, peace of mind

Shalom Aleichem – Yiddish writer who lived from 1859-1916

Shehehayanu – blessing for beginnings and happy occasions

Shofar – a ram's horn blown at Rosh Hashanah and Yom Kippur, also, at important times in Ancient Israel

Tallit – a prayer shawl that has fringes

Temple, the – place of worship in ancient Jerusalem; First Temple destroyed by Babylonians and the Second Temple destroyed by Romans

Torah – the first five books of the Bible

Tzedakah – charity or the act of doing good deeds and helping the poor

Wailing Wall – the last part of the wall from the Temple of Jerusalem, same as Western Wall

Yahrzeit – the date of death of a family member

Yizkor – memorial prayer for the dead

TERMS

Substitutions

For Passover substitute 1 cup flour with 1/4 cup matzo cake meal and 3/4 cup potato starch.

Weights and Measurements

3 teaspoons	=	1 Tablespoon	=	1/2 fluid ounce
4 Tablespoons	=	1/4 cup	=	2 fluid ounces
5 1/3 Tablespoons	=	1/3 cup	=	2.7 fluid ounces
8 Tablespoons	=	1 cup	=	8 fluid ounces
2 cups	=	1 pint	=	16 fluid ounces
2 pints	=	1 quart	=	32 fluid ounces
4 cups	=	1 quart	=	32 fluid ounces
4 quarts	=	1 gallon	=	64 fluid ounces

Metric

American		Metric		Rounded Metric
1 teaspoon	=	4.9 milliliters	=	5 ml
1 Tablespoon	=	14.8 milliliters	=	15 ml
1 cup	=	236.6 milliliters	=	240 ml
1 quart	=	946.4 milliliters	=	950 ml
1.06 quart	=	1 liter	=	1 l
1 ounce	=	28.35 grams	=	30 g
4 ounces	=	113.4 grams	=	115 g
1 pound	=	453.59 grams	=	454 g
2.2 pounds	=	1000 grams	=	1 kg
250°F	=	90°C		
350°F	=	180°C		
375°F	=	190°C		
400°F	=	200°C		
425°F	=	220°C		
450°F	=	230°C		

TERMS

*R*ESOURCES

Selected Sources To Consult

PART I: READINGS

With so many books written on Judaism selecting a few good ones is difficult. For the most part, the list below and readings listed after the holidays is a sampling based upon the School Library Journal or Library Journal reviews. Reading levels are given.

General

Clap and Count!: Action Rhymes for the Jewish Year
by Jacqueline Jules, Sally Springer (Illustrator), ages 3 mo. to 6 yrs.

A Child's First Book of Jewish Holidays
by Alfred J. Kolatch, Harry Araten (Illustrator), ages 4-8

A Sweet Year: A Taste of the Jewish Holidays
by Mark Podwal, ages 4-8

Dance, Sing, Remember: A Celebration of Jewish Holidays
by Leslie Kimmelman , Ora Eitan (Illustrator), ages 4-8

The Family Treasury of Jewish Holidays
by Malka Drucker, ages 9-12

Holiday Tales
by Sholom Aleichem (Author), Aliza Shevrin (Editor), ages 9-12

Jewish Family & Life: Traditions, Holidays, and Values for Today's Parents and Children
by Yosef I. Abramowitz, Susan Silverman, adult

Series

Sammy Spider's for ages 4-12 depending on the book, each book relates to a special holiday

Bina, Benny and Chaggai Hayonah for ages 9-12, each book relates to a holiday

Crafts

Jewish Holiday Craft Book
by Kathy Ross, Melinda Levine (Illustrator), preschool to gr 5

Jewish Holiday Crafts for Little Hands
by Ruth Esrig Brinn, Katherine Kahn (Illustrator), ages 9-12

History

Cultures of the Jews : A New History
by David Biale, adult

Jews, God, and History
by Max I. Dimont, adult

A History of the Jews
by Paul Johnson, adult

RESOURCES

PART II : WEB SITES

www.urj.com formally www.uahc Union of Reform Judaism

www.rossel.net rabbi provides basics about holidays and
practices

www.myjewishbooksonline.com lists 100 best Jewish books,
award winner

www.koretfoundation.org lists awards for best Jewish writing

www.jewishbookmall.com software, books, music

www.everythingjewish.com holidays, laws, family fun, recipes,
shopping

www.judaism.com books, music, videos, gifts, religious items

www.torahtots.com lots of activities for kids, conservative
bend on holidays

PART III: HOLIDAY BIBLIOGRAPHY

Burstein, Chaya. *The Jewish Kids Catalog*. Philadelphia: The
Jewish Publication Society America, 1984.

Encyclopedia Judaica. Jerusalem: Keter Publishing House, 1974.

Epstein, Morris. *All About Jewish Holidays and Customs*. KTAV
Publication House, Inc., 1970.

RESOURCES

Fellner, Judith B. *In the Jewish Tradition: A Year of Food and Festivities.* New York: Micharel Friedman Publishing Group, Inc., 1995.

Fox, Karen L. and Phyllis Zimbler Miller. *Seasons for Celebration: A Contemporary Guide to the Joys, Practices, and Traditions of the Jewish Holidays.* New York: Perigee, 1992.

Gates of Repentance – The New Union Prayerbook for the Days of Awe. New York: Central Conference of American Rabbis, 1996.

Klagsbrun, Francine. *Jewish Days – A Book of Life and Culture Around the Year.* New York: The Noonday Press, 1996.

Kotatch, Alfred. *The Jewish Book of Why.* New York: Jonathan David Publishers, Inc., 1981.

Stern, Shirley. *Exploring the Prayerbook.* KTAV Publishing House, Inc., 1983.

Telushkin, Joseph. *Jewish Literacy.* New York: William Morrow and Company, Inc., 1991.

Waskow, Arthur. *Seasons of Our Joy: A Modern Guide to the Jewish Holidays.* Boston: Beacon, 1982.

Weber, Vicki L. (ed). *Rhythm of Jewish Life: An Introduction to Holidays and Life-Cycle Events.* New Jersey: Behrman House, 1999.

www.angelfire.com/pa2/passover<http://www.angelfire.com/pa2/passover> (20 Jan. 2004)

RESOURCES

CHAROSET

Sephardic Charoset (P)

Barbara Weinberg

1/2 cup almonds
1/2 cup walnuts
8 ounces pitted dates, halved
about 1/4 cup sweet wine
3/4 teaspoon ground ginger
1/2 teaspoon ground cinnamon
pinch freshly ground black pepper
2 pinches ground cloves
1 medium apple, cored

1. Finely chop almonds and walnuts in food processor. Remove to mixing bowl.
2. Place dates, wine, ginger, cinnamon, pepper and cloves in food processor. Process until fairly smooth. Add to nuts. Mix well.
3. Grate apple coarsely and stir in. Add more wine if necessary to make a mixture that is spreadable but still thick.

Makes: 1 3/4 cups

▤Passover dish

▤Charoset is a mixture of fruits and nuts chopped to resemble mortar. It is served at the Passover seder to symbolize the mortar used by the Israelite slaves to build the Egyptian pyramids. The regional flavors vary with the ingredients available to the settlers: Ashkenazic charoset has a large proportion of apples; Sephardic, mid-eastern, has a generous amount of dates; Yemenite has dates, figs and hot pepper and an updated American version has mango.

Ashkenazic Charoset (P)

Barbara Weinberg

3 ounces (3/4 cup) walnuts
1/4 large cooking apple
kosher wine to moisten
2 teaspoons cinnamon
2 teaspoons sugar

1. Mince walnuts and apple. (You can use a food processor for this.)
2. Moisten with kosher wine. The consistency should be that of mortar!
3. Add cinnamon and sugar. Mix well.

Makes: 20 very small (1/2 teaspoon) servings

Passover dish

American Mango Charoset (P)

Barbara Weinberg

2 Granny Smith apples
Juice of half a lemon, about 1 Tablespoon
1/2 cup fresh mango, peeled and diced
1/2 cup chopped toasted pecans
1/2 teaspoon cinnamon
1 Tablespoon honey
1 Tablespoon Port or sweet wine

1. Peel, core, and dice the apples. Sprinkle diced apples with lemon juice.
2. Place all ingredients in a food processor. Pulse once or twice just to break up. Place in bowl, cover and let sit in refrigerator for the flavors to meld.

Makes: About 2 Cups

Passover dish

Almond-Date Charoset (P)

Deborah Achtenberg

1/2 cup pitted dates
1 cup boiling water
1 cup (about 5 oz.) whole blanched almonds
3 Tablespoons sweet white wine
1 Tablespoon poppy seeds
1 teaspoon finely grated lemon zest
1 teaspoon ground ginger

1. Cook dates in boiling water until plump, about 3 minutes, or microwave at full power for 1 minute.)
2. Drain dates, reserving 1/4 cup of the cooking liquid.
3. Put dates, reserved liquid and almonds in food processor bowl with steel knives. Pulse until finely chopped.
4. Transfer to a bowl and stir in the wine, poppy seeds, lemon zest and ginger.
5. Serve chilled or at room temperature.

Makes: 1 cup

✍I love the traditional European charoset with apples and walnuts, but it's nice to have this tasty Middle-Eastern one, too! It's from Eden Ross Lipson's Passover dinner. I make it every year.

✓If you want to prepare ahead, cover and refrigerate for up to 2 days. Muscat wine works well, too.

▤Passover dish

Yemenite Charoset (P)

Barbara Weinberg

1 cup pitted chopped dates
1/2 cup chopped dried figs
1/3 cup sweet Passover wine
3 Tablespoons sesame seeds
1 teaspoon ground ginger
pinch coriander
1 small red chili pepper, seeded and minced OR pinch
    of cayenne
2 Tablespoons matzo meal

1. Combine dates, figs and wine. Add sesame seeds, ginger, coriander, red chili pepper and matzo meal. Blend thoroughly.
2. Roll into 1-inch balls or serve in a bowl.

Makes: 1 1/2 cups

✓ A heavier fruit flavor with dates and figs and spiced hot with ginger and red chili pepper.

▤ Passover dish

Jonathan, age 10

APPETIZERS

Artichoke Dip (D)

Helene Paris

1 can (8 1/2 oz.) artichoke hearts in water
1 cup grated Parmesan cheese
1/2 cup mayonnaise
1/2 cup sour cream
1 package (8 oz.) cream cheese, softened
dill weed, to taste
garlic salt, to taste

1. Drain and chop artichoke.
2. Add all remaining ingredients. Mix together well. Spread in a greased ovenproof serving dish.
3. Bake at 350°F for 20 minutes or until light brown and bubbly. Serve hot.

Makes about 3 cups

Oven: 350°F   Bake Time: 20 min.

▤Passover Recipe

▤Globe Artichokes, as in the above recipe, are a Mediterranean native resembling a thistle. We eat the flower bud of the plant. The "petals" are pulled off and the soft meaty inner portion is scrapped off and eaten. The hard "petal" is discarded as is the fuzzy choke. The artichoke heart is the meaty central part minus the fuzzy choke. It is available canned and frozen.

▤Jerusalem artichoke or sunchoke is a tuber of a sunflower that grows six to twelve feet tall. It has a white flesh, is crisp and the taste resembles globe artichokes. Italian for sunflower is *girasole* which may have become Jerusalem but it did not come from Jerusalem. In fact, it is a native of North America.

Cold Vegetable Pizza (D)

Linda Kutten

2 tubes (8 oz. each) refrigerated crescent rolls
2 packages (8 oz. each) cream cheese, softened
1/2 cup mayonnaise
1/2 envelope (about 0.7 oz.) dry dressing mix (Italian or
    Ranch)
6 mushrooms, sliced
1 head broccoli, flowerets cut bite-size
1 head cauliflower, flowerets cut bite-size
1 can (15 oz.) olives, drained and halved
2 carrots, grated
8 oz. shredded Monterey Jack cheese

1. Preheat oven to 375°F. Roll out crescent roll dough to fit
    16x11-inch cookie sheet. Pinch and pat to seal rolls to
    each other. Bake at 375°F for 10 minutes or until
    browned. Cool thoroughly.
2. Meanwhile, combine cream cheese, mayonnaise and
    dressing mix. Spread on cooled crust.
3. Arrange on top of cream cheese mixture the remaining
    ingredients in the order listed. Cover with foil or plastic
    wrap. Press down to secure vegetables onto pizza.
    Refrigerate 2 hours or more.
4. To serve, slice into 1 1/2x2-inch pieces. Be sure to cut all
    the way through.

Makes 35 slices

Oven: 375°F   Bake Time: 10 min.   Refrigerate: 2 hours

✓There are a lot of vegetables on the pizza. Keeping the
vegetables in small bite-size pieces is easier for the eater and
the cutter.

Lox (Smoked Salmon) Pizza (D)

Linda Kutten

1 tube (10 oz.) refrigerator pizza crust
1 package (8 oz.) cream cheese, softened
1 package (3 oz.) thinly sliced smoked salmon (lox)
1/2 medium red onion, thinly sliced
1 tomato, thinly sliced
1 to 2 Tablespoons capers

1. Form pizza crust into 12x9-inch rectangle. Bake at 400°F for 10 minutes till browned. Cool.
2. Spread softened cream cheese over cooled crust.
3. Lay slices of salmon over cream cheese with space between strips. Follow with onion and tomato. The onion and tomato slices may be cut into quarters so that they fit on top of the salmon, making the final cutting of the pizza easier.
4. Sprinkle with capers. Cover with plastic wrap and refrigerate until ready to serve.
5. To serve: Cut into 1 1/2x2-inch slices.

Makes about 25 pieces

Herring Hors D'oeuvres (P)

Beatrice N. Brown

1 jar (2 pounds) herring tidbits in wine sauce
1 jar Bennet's® chili sauce only
1 red pepper, cut up
1 green pepper, cut up
1 purple onion, cut up

1. Drain herring, leaving a little juice and a few onions.
2. Mix all ingredients together. Refrigerate. Make one week ahead.

Melding time: one week   ▤Passover Recipe

APPETIZERS

Salmon Smoosh (D)

Julie Stage

1 can (15 oz.) salmon, drained, skin and bones removed
1 package (8 oz.) cream cheese, at room temperature
2 Tablespoons grated onion
1 Tablespoon lemon juice
pinch of smoked salt
ground pepper to taste
chopped parsley or walnuts

Garnishes
cucumber slices
tomato slices
red onion rings
black and green olives

1. Combine salmon, cream cheese, onion, and lemon juice. Blend well. Season with smoked salt and pepper to taste.
2. Chill until firm enough to shape, about 30 minutes.
3. Using waxed paper or aluminum foil, shape in a cylinder and roll in parsley or chopped walnuts.
4. Chill 8 hours or overnight. To serve garnish with items mentioned above. Serve with pita chips, bagels or matzo.

Chill Time: 8 hours or overnight

▤Passover Recipe

✓If you like to be creative and play with your food, shape the paté freehand into the form of a fish and decorate it with olive and pimento slices or cucumber slices to look like scales then a black olive slice for eyes, etc.

✓ You can use the low fat variety of cream cheese— but do NOT use fat-free or it turns to soup.

Mushroom Turnovers (D)

Sharon Honig-Bear

Dough
9 ounces cream cheese, softened
1/2 cup butter, softened
1 1/2 cups flour
Mushroom Filling
1 large onion, finely chopped
3 Tablespoons butter
8 ounces mushrooms, finely chopped
1/4 teaspoon thyme
1/2 teaspoon salt
Pepper
2 Tablespoons flour
1/4 cup sweet or sour cream

1. *For dough*: Mix cream cheese and butter thoroughly with mixer, food processor or by hand. Add flour and work lightly. Divide in 2-3 sections, flatten each slightly and cover each with plastic wrap or waxed paper. Refrigerate at least one hour (can be left refrigerated for several days or frozen for longer).
2. *For filling*: In skillet, sauté onion in butter for several minutes. Add mushrooms. Cook about 3 more minutes. Add seasonings, sprinkle with flour and heat for a minute or two. Add cream. Stir until thickened. Set aside.
3. Roll dough to 1/8-inch thick on lightly floured surface and cut into 3-inch rounds (use a small glass).
4. Place approximately 1/2 teaspoon of the mushroom filling in each and fold over to form turnover. Press edges together with fork.
5. Bake at 450°F on ungreased baking sheet 15 minutes or until lightly browned.

Makes: 2 dozen

Oven: 450°F   Bake Time: 15 min

APPETIZERS

Spinach Balls (D)

Julie Stage

6 eggs
2 packages (10 oz. each) frozen spinach, thawed
2 cups herbed stuffing mix
1 large onion, grated
1 cup Parmesan cheese
3/4 cup margarine, room temperature
1 teaspoon poultry seasoning
salt and pepper to taste

1.   In large bowl, beat eggs lightly. Add remaining
     ingredients, blend well.
2.   Roll mixture into walnut-size balls. Place on cookie sheets
     sprayed with cooking oil spray.
3.   Bake at 350°F for 20 minutes. Serve hot.

Makes: 6 dozen

Oven: 350°F   Bake Time: 20 min.

✓These are great to make ahead and freeze. To freeze: Allow to
cool 10 minutes. Freeze in airtight container. Reheat in 350°F
oven for 10-15 minutes.

✔These days spinach is so easy to prepare. Before the days of
bagged spinach leaves, spinach was in bunches and had to be
rinsed and rinsed to be sure to get all of the sand out. The flat
or smooth leaf spinach are easier to clean than the savoy which
has crinkly, curly leaves. The flat leaf spinach is usually canned
or frozen.

✔Select bagged spinach that are not matted together. If
selecting bunches, look for thin stems, no yellow spots, a fresh
sweet smell--not sour or musty.

Moroccan Meatballs (M)

Linda Kutten

Meatballs
1 pound very lean ground beef
2 teaspoons garlic powder
1/4 cup matzo meal
1 egg
1 teaspoon cumin

Sauce
2 teaspoons cumin
1 teaspoon hot paprika
1 teaspoon paprika
1 cup water
juice of one lemon

1. Mix together all ingredients for meatballs. Roll into 3/4-inch diameter balls.
2. Combine all sauce ingredients in large skillet. Heat to boiling.
3. Add meatballs. Meatballs should be in single layer. Cover skillet. Simmer about 20 minutes until meatballs are cooked through. Be sure to stir meatballs at least once to coat with sauce. Serve hot.

Makes about 47, 3/4-inch balls

▤ Passover Recipe

✓ May be made the day ahead and just reheated in microwave oven. Or can be formed into balls, frozen and reheated when needed.

APPETIZERS

Cheese and Apricot Log (D)

Kathryn Karp

8 ounces cream cheese, at room temperature
1/4 cup white wine
1/4 teaspoon salt
16 ounces sharp Cheddar cheese, shredded
1 teaspoon caraway seeds
1/2 cup dried apricots, finely chopped

1. Beat cream cheese, wine, and salt together until fluffy.
2. Blend in Cheddar cheese, caraway and apricots. Refrigerate 30 minutes.
3. Turn out onto a sheet of foil. Shape into a roll. Wrap in foil and chill at least 2 hours or overnight.
4. Serve with pumpernickel or crackers.

Makes 1 log   ▤Passover Recipe

Preparation Time: 30 min.   Chill time before serving: 2 hr

Gourmet Brie (D)

Lisa Lowhurst

1 wedge of Brie (or circle)
8 Tablespoons toasted pine nuts, coarsely chopped
5 Tablespoons chopped fresh parsley
10 sun dried tomatoes in oil, drained a bit and chopped
2 1/2 Tablespoons oil from sun dried tomatoes
5 cloves garlic, chopped and minced
2 Tablespoons chopped fresh basil

1. Trim rind off Brie. Place trimmed Brie on serving plate.
2. Chop and mix together all remaining ingredients. Pour over Brie. Let sit at room temperature for 30 to 60 minutes before serving.

Melding Time: 30-60 min.   ▤Passover Recipe

APPETIZERS

BRUNCH

Chicken Liver Pâté (M)

Ruth Dickens

2 Tablespoons schmaltz (rendered chicken fat)
1 carton (1 pound) fresh chicken liver, cleaned
1 medium onion, cut up
Kosher salt & pepper to taste
3 hard cooked eggs, shelled & quartered

1. In large skillet over medium heat, heat the schmaltz. Add livers and onions, sautéing until livers are thoroughly cooked. Sprinkle with salt and pepper.
2. Put liver mixture, including fat, through food grinder (not blender or food processor), using fine blade. If mixture is not moist enough, add little more schmaltz. Mix together all ingredients well. Serve as spread on buffet rye or crackers.

Makes about 3 cups

▤Passover Recipe

✓To render chicken fat: Place raw cut-up chicken fat in skillet with cover over low heat. Cook until fat is rendered. Add a chopped onion to fat; continue cooking until onions are golden brown. Drain through sieve into a heat-proof container. Store in refrigerator or freezer. It will keep indefinitely in freezer.

▤CHOPPED LIVER. We can never have enough chopped liver recipes. Each has a different twist and a story. The basic ingredients are chopped chicken livers, onion, and hard cooked eggs. Traditionally, rendered chicken fat (schmaltz) is used to cook the livers and to moisten the mix. (See above on rendering chicken fat.) The French pâté evolved from the chopped liver.

Zaudy Family's German Chopped Liver (M)

Richard & Patricia Eisenberg

1 cup rendered chicken fat or butter
1 large onion, finely chopped
2 pounds chicken liver
salt
pepper
garlic powder
6 hard cooked eggs, peeled

1. Heat rendered chicken fat or butter in large skillet until very hot. Stir in onion. Sauté until onion is clear and soft, lowering cooking heat as needed to prevent browning.
2. Bring pan up to medium heat. Add chicken liver and cook until done. Liver will be lightly browned all the way through.
3. Season to taste with salt, pepper and garlic powder. Remove from heat.
4. Put liver mixture and eggs into food processor. Process until completely chopped and slightly creamy. Season again to taste.
5. Serve chilled, mounded in the center of a large platter over a bed of lettuce and surrounded with rye crackers.

Makes about 6 cups

▤Passover Recipe

✍This recipe is Richard's mother's family's from Berlin, Germany.

✓A blender or French knife may be used in place of a food processor to chop the liver and eggs.

✍ In olden days, the liver was chopped in a big rounded wooden chopping bowl by a hand held chopper. The blade of the chopper was curved to fit the contours of the bowl. The bowl was held steady in the cutters lap

Grandmother's Chopped Liver (M)

Emmy Bell

> 3 to 6 onions, chopped
> chicken fat
> 1 pound chicken livers, washed and dried
> 3 hard cooked eggs, peeled and chopped

1. Sauté onions in chicken fat until brown but not crunchy. Put into chopping bowl.
2. Cook chicken livers in frying pan over medium heat until no blood shows and they are brown throughout. Add to chopping bowl. Chop liver and onions together.
3. Add chopped hard cooked eggs and chop a little more. Salt and pepper to taste. Serve warm or chilled.

Makes about 3 cups   ▤Passover Recipe

Chopped Liver with Mushrooms and Wine (M)

Helene Paris

> 3 large onions, chopped
> 2 Tablespoons vegetable oil
> 1 pound chicken livers
> 1 jar (4-oz.) mushrooms stems and pieces, drained
> 3 Tablespoons wine
> 7 to 8 hard cooked eggs, peeled
> salt and pepper, to taste

1. Fry onions in vegetable oil until brown. Add liver and mushrooms. Cook until brown.
2. Add wine and steam with lid on for 15 minutes.
3. Put the mixture through a grinder or food processor with the eggs, salt and pepper, grinding all lumps.
4. Mold the liver by hand or put into a mold to shape.
5. Serve with rye bread cut into quarters or on small rye rounds.

Makes about 4 cups   ▤Passover Recipe

Peas "Chopped Liver" (P)

Helene Paris

4 medium onions, chopped
1 Tablespoon vegetable oil
1 cup finely chopped walnuts
4 to 5 hard cooked eggs
1 can (15 oz.) very young small early peas, drained

1. In skillet, sauté onions in oil. Set aside.
2. In food processor, chop walnuts until almost fine. Remove to mixing bowl.
3. Process each of the following ingredients separately, removing contents to chopped walnuts bowl each time: eggs, peas and sautéed onions.
4. Stir together all chopped ingredients. If needed, use oil from sautéed onions to make mixture softer.

Makes 4 cups

▤Passover Recipe

✓ To cut down on cholesterol, use 2 whole eggs and 3 egg whites only. I use Le Seur® canned peas.

▤MOCK CHOPPED LIVER. In recent years we have become more conscious of the high cholesterol in liver. To be able to taste chopped liver yet not have it present in the recipe has produced many imitations included in the cookbook. Try them, you'll be surprised.

Celery and Walnut "Chopped Liver" (P)

Nadine Lipson

    1 cup minced celery
    2 onions, minced
    1/4 cup oil
    12 hard cooked eggs, chopped
    8 ounces ground walnuts
    salt and pepper

1. In skillet, sauté celery and onions in oil until dark. Cool.
2. Add eggs and walnuts to sautéed vegetables and chop well. Season to taste with salt and pepper.

Makes about 4 cups

▤Passover Recipe

Green Beans "Chopped Liver" (P)

Helene Paris

    1 medium onion, sliced
    1 Tablespoon vegetable oil
    1 can (15 oz.) cut green beans, drained
    1/2 cup chopped walnuts
    2 hard cooked eggs
    salt & pepper to taste

1. Lightly brown onions in oil.
2. Process remaining ingredients in food processor until fine.
3. Add onions. Pulse food processor to chop onions. Chill. Serve on lettuce leaves.

Makes 2 cups

▤Passover Recipe

Eggplant & Lentil "Chopped Liver" (P)

Linda Kutten

1 medium eggplant (1 1/4 lbs.), peeled and sliced
1/3 cup green lentils
1 cup and 1 cup finely chopped onions
1 1/2 cups (8 oz.) coarsely chopped mushrooms
1 Tablespoon olive oil
2 Tablespoons balsamic vinegar
2 large cloves garlic, cut up
1/2 teaspoon ground white pepper
1 cup egg substitute
2 large egg whites
6 large hard-cooked eggs, whites only
1/4 cup toasted walnuts
1/4 cup mayonnaise

1. Place eggplant on baking sheet. Spray with olive oil cooking spray. Broil until lightly browned. Turn over, spray with oil and broil until browned.
2. Cook lentils in 1 cup water for 20 minutes untill soft. Drain.
3. Sauté 1 cup chopped onion and mushrooms in oil until soft. Stir in drained lentils; vinegar; garlic; and pepper.
4. Mix together egg substitute and whites. Cover and cook over low heat in nonstick skillet for about 10 minutes or until firm but not browned.
5. Place in food processor container with steel blade the browned eggplant, cut in quarters; onion-lentil mixture; cooked eggs, cut-up; remaining 1 cup finely chopped raw onions; hard-cooked egg whites, cut-up; and walnuts. Pulse until blended and uniformly minced.
6. Stir in mayonnaise and adjust seasoning with salt and pepper. Cover. Refrigerate several hours or overnight before serving with matzo crackers.

Makes about 4 cups   ▤Passover Recipe

Cheese Bourrekas (Cheese Turnovers) (D)

Kathryn Karp

Filling
8 ounces cream cheese
8 ounces feta cheese
1 egg
1/2 teaspoon salt

Dough
1 heaping teaspoon baking powder
4 cups flour
8 ounces margarine, unsalted
1/3 cup, 1/3 cup and 1/3 cup milk
1 egg yolk, beaten
sesame seeds

1. *For Filling*: Combine all filling ingredients. Set aside.
2. *For Dough*: Add baking powder to flour. Cut in margarine until mixture looks like meal. Divide into three portions
3. Combine 1/3 cup milk with 1/3 of the flour mixture and knead lightly into a ball. Roll out into a small sheet. Cut into twenty 3-inch rounds and fill with a heaping teaspoon of cheese filling. Fold rounds in half and pinch together in a ruffled pattern. Place on baking sheet. Brush with beaten egg yolk and sprinkle with sesame seeds.
4. Repeat step 3 two more times.
5. Bake at 350°F for 20 minutes or until bourrekas are light golden in color.

Makes 60 bourrekas

Oven: 350°F   Bake Time: 20 min.

✓ By mixing the dough in three portions, the dough is not sticky as only a small amount is being handled at a time.

📖BOURREKAS are crisp short crust pastry of Turkish origin.

Knishes

Knishes are baked pastry pockets traditionally filled with potato. But they can be filled with cheese, meat, spinach, cabbage or even chopped liver. The size varies from mini appetizer size to a huge hamburger size. Some even serve it with an *au jus* dip.

Tips from Debbie Baer:

✓The dough is quite thin, yet pliable. It is tricky to seal the ends, but keep trying! My mom has the secret touch for delicious potato knishes. As a young girl, I remember helping her seal the ends of each one. I've had plenty of practice now, so I am a great Potato Knish "sealer."

✓If you have any mashed potato mixture left over, you can always serve them separately!

✓I always prepare the knishes in advance, using 10 pounds of potatoes, triple the dough recipe and devote most of the day making knishes. This gives me tons in my freezer, ready to serve.

✓Freeze on cookie sheets then store in plastic freezer bags. To serve, just pull out amount desired. Bake from frozen state at 350°F for 30 minutes.

Other Tips:

✓For more flavor in filling, add chopped parsley or sautéed chopped mushrooms.

✓To make large knishes: Divide the mini potato knish dough into 4 pieces. Roll each piece out into a 7-inch circle. Mound 1 cup filling in center; bring dough up around sides, leaving the center exposed. Bake in 425°F oven for 25 to 30 minutes.

✓As a time saver, instead of making the pastry, use the frozen prepared puff pastry. Everyone at the Sisterhood knish cooking lesson loved the results and the ease of preparation.

Potato Knishes (P)

Debbie Baer

Filling
approximately 3 1/3 pounds potatoes
2 onions, chopped
salt and pepper

Dough
1 egg
1/2 cup vegetable oil
1/2 cup hot water
pinch salt
2 heaping Tablespoons baking powder
2 cups flour

1. *For filling*: Boil and mash potatoes. Sauté onions until rich brown. Add to mashed potatoes and let cool.
2. *For dough*: Mix all dough ingredients together and divide into two balls.
3. On a floured board, roll one ball into a "stretched oval" shape. The dough should be quite thin. Slice the dough in half, lengthwise. Spread a long line of potatoes on each half of the dough. (You may wish to add a little salt and pepper to the potatoes at this point.) Rolling from the center out, cover the line of potatoes with dough and keep on rolling to the outside. You should now have two long rolls. Repeat this with the second ball of dough.
4. Slice each roll into approximately 1 1/2-inch pieces. Using your fingers, try to pinch the dough on each side of each piece to seal the knishes.
5. Bake on cookie sheets at 350°F for about 20-30 minutes or until they are lightly browned.

Makes 15 servings

Oven: 350°F   Bake Time: 20-30 min.

Mini Potato Knishes (D)

Linda Kutten

Potato Filling
1/2 large onion, finely chopped
1 Tablespoons olive oil
2 Tablespoons butter
1 lb potatoes, peeled, chunked, cooked, mashed
1/4 teaspoon salt
1/8 teaspoon white pepper
1 egg white (reserve egg yolk for egg wash)

Pastry
2 cups flour
1/2 teaspoon salt
1/4 cup butter, cut into chunks
3 Tablespoons shortening
6 to 10 Tablespoons ice water

1. On Low cook chopped onion in olive oil and butter until golden, about 20 minutes. Stir in mashed potatoes, salt. pepper and egg white. Chill.
4. *To make pastry:* In food processor bowl, pulse flour, salt, butter and shortening until coarse crumbs form. Add 6 tablespoons water, pulse to mix. Add water, one tablespoon at a time, until mixture begins to hold together. Form into ball. Wrap. Chill.
5. *To assemble knishes:* Roll half the dough to 8x12-inch. Cut in half lengthwise. Place a strip of potato down the center of both strips. Fold sides to enclose filling. Slice 1 1/2-inch pieces. Pinch the two cut ends closed. Round knish to shape. Dip one end into egg wash mixture of yolk and 1 Tablespoon water. Place on parchment lined cookie sheets with dipped end up. Bake at 425°F for 20 to 25 minutes, until browned on top.

Makes: 32 mini knishes.

Oven: 425°F   Bake Time: 20 to 25 min.

Mom's Version of Kishka (M)

Nancy Daum

2 cups matzo meal
1 cup flour
1 cup margarine, melted
1 3/4 teaspoons seasoned salt
1 cup chicken broth

1. Combine all ingredients.
2. Shape into two logs 10 inches long. Wrap each in foil.
3. Bake on a cookie sheet at 350°F for 30-40 minutes. Unwrap, slice about 1/2-inch thick and serve.

Makes 30 slices   ▤Passover Recipe

Oven: 350°F   Bake Time: 30-40 min.

Mock Derma (Kishka) (D)

Helene Paris

2-3 carrots, grated
2-3 stalks of celery, grated
1 medium onion, grated
1 box (8 oz.) miniature matzo crackers (Tam Tam)
1 stick (4 oz.) butter, melted

1. Grind all together with melted butter. Mix thoroughly.
2. Make two 10-inch logs. Wrap each in foil.
3. Bake on cookie sheet at 350°F for 40 minutes. Unwrap, slice about 1/2-inch thick and serve.

Makes 4 – 6 servings   ▤Passover Recipe

Oven: 350°F   Bake Time: 40 min.

▤KISHKA is stuffed derma or skin shaped like a sausage. The casing was intestines, or chicken neck skin; stuffed with matzo mixture and cooked on top of the cholent, like a dumpling. Now we just wrap in foil and bake.

Falafel (P)

Tinia Merkin

1 1/4 cups dried chickpeas
3 cloves garlic
1 teaspoon cumin seed
1 teaspoon coriander seed
pinch of finely chopped cilantro
handful of flat leaf parsley, chopped
1/4 teaspoon chili powder
1 teaspoon salt
1 Tablespoon lemon juice
ground black pepper
1 teaspoon baking powder
oil for frying
pita bread & hummus to serve

1. Soak chickpeas overnight.
2. Drain chickpeas, discarding water. Place chickpeas in food processor. Process until chickpeas are broken up.
3. Crush garlic. Grind cumin and coriander seeds.
4. Add to chickpeas garlic, cumin, coriander, cilantro, parsley, chili powder and salt. Process until smooth.
5. Add lemon juice and black pepper to taste. Add more spices, if desired. Let stand 30 minutes to blend flavors.
6. Stir in baking powder. Form into small balls.
7. Fry in hot oil until falafel is golden. Drain and serve with pita bread and warm hummus.

Makes: 18 small balls, enough for 4 servings

Overnight Time: Soak beans   Melding Time: 30 min.

FALAFEL, a mid-eastern favorite, is ground chickpeas formed in balls or patties and deep-fried.

Matzo Brei (D)

Gil Gafni

2 matzos
milk to cover
6 eggs
salt to taste

oil or butter, just enough to coat skilletmaple syrup

1. Crumble matzo in bowl. Cover with milk. Let sit for 30 minutes.
2. In another bowl, beat eggs. Add salt and pepper to taste.
3. Drain milk from matzos. Squeeze matzos dry. Add to eggs. Mix well.
4. Heat oil in skillet. Add matzo-egg mixture. Scramble. Serve drizzled with maple syrup.

Makes 4 servings

Soaking Time: 30 min.   Cook Time: about 4 min.

📑Passover Recipe

✓Instead of soaking the matzos in milk, water may be used.

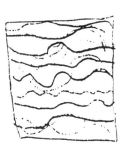 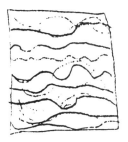

Jack, age 8

📑MATZO BREI is matzo fried with eggs. The dish is served a lot during Passover

Mashed Potato Muffins (D)

Elizabeth Kempler

2 eggs, separated
2 cups mashed potatoes
1 medium onion, diced
1 Tablespoon butter, melted
1/2 cup milk
1/2 cup matzo meal
Salt to taste

1. Preheat oven to 375°F.
2. Beat egg whites until soft peaks. Set aside.
3. Mix together egg yolks, potatoes, onion, butter, milk, matzo flour and salt.
4. Butter muffin tins and fill half full.
5. Spread beaten egg whites over potato mixture.
6. Bake at 375°F for 15 minutes or until tops are browned.

Makes 12 muffins

Oven: 375°F   Bake Time: about 15 min.

📋 Passover Recipe

✍ This is a German family recipe that's over 100 years old and is great for Passover. Egg white foam crowns the muffins.

📋 Matzo is thin unleavened bread, like a flat cracker, made from only flour and water. This is the only bread eaten during Passover. Matzo comes in different shapes for use in Passover cooking: chunks like confetti - matzo farfel, size of cornmeal - matzo meal, and finer yet - matzo cake flour.

Challah Soufflé (D)

Linda Kutten

> 6 eggs
> 1 cup milk
> pinch cayenne
> 1 1/2 cups grated sharp cheddar cheese
> 1/2 loaf challah, cut in 1-inch cubes
> salt and white pepper to taste

1. In a large bowl beat together well eggs, milk and cayenne.
2. In bottom of a 9x9-inch baking dish, spread 1/2 cup of cheese. Cover with half of the challah. Sprinkle with salt and pepper to taste. Layer 1/2 cup cheese then remaining challah and topping with last 1/2 cup cheese. Pour egg mixture over all. Let sit 10 minutes while oven preheats to 350°F.
3. Bake at 350°F for 45 minutes until puffed and golden.

Makes 4 servings

Oven: 350°F   Bake Time: 45 min.

Stuffed French Toast (D)

Pam Sloan

9 eggs
2 cups milk
1/2 cup maple syrup
1 loaf French sourdough bread, sliced
1 package (8 oz.) cream cheese, softened
cinnamon

1. In a large bowl, beat together well eggs, milk and maple syrup.
2. In bottom of a 9x13-inch well-greased baking dish, lay bread slices in a single layer to cover bottom. Spread cream cheese over slices. Cut the remaining bread slices into cubes. Spread cubes over cream cheese. Pour egg mixture over cubes. Sprinkle cinnamon over top. Cover and refrigerate overnight.
3. Bake at 350°F for 55 minutes. Cut into squares and serve drizzled with hot buttered maple syrup topped with powdered sugar.

Makes 8 servings

Sit overnight in refrigerator.

Oven: 350°F   Bake Time: 55 min.

✓For hot buttered maple syrup heat 1/2 cup maple syrup with 1/4 cup butter.

✓For a variation try peanut butter instead of cream cheese and add sliced bananas.

Hot 6-Fruits with Walnut Topping (D or P)

Zoe Rose

1 can (29 oz.) pineapple chunks, drained
1 can (29 oz.) peaches, drained
1 can (29 oz.) sliced pears, drained
1 can (29 oz.) apricots, drained
2 bananas
1 can (21 oz.) cherry pie filling
1/2 cup white wine

Topping
6 Tablespoons flour
4 Tablespoons butter or margarine
3/4 cup chopped walnuts
1/2 cup firmly packed brown sugar
2 Tablespoons cinnamon

1. In 13x9-inch baking pan, arrange pineapple, peaches, pears, and apricots.
2. Slice bananas over top.
3. Pour cherry filling and wine over all.
4. Combine topping ingredients and crumble over top.
5. Bake at 350°F for 30 minutes.

Makes about 16 servings

Oven: 350°F   Bake Time: 30 min.

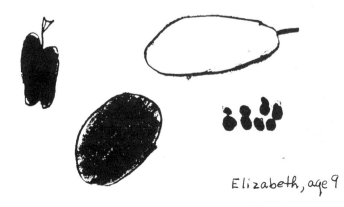

Elizabeth, age 9

Hot 7-Fruit Compote (P)

Pam Sloan

1 can (29 oz.) pineapple chunks
1 can (29 oz.) pitted dark sweet cherries
1 can (29 oz.) pear halves
1 can (29 oz.) apricot halves
16 peaches, sliced
2 tart apples, cored, diced
3 Tablespoons lemon juice
1/2 teaspoon ground nutmeg
1/2 teaspoon cinnamon
1/4 teaspoon ground cloves
1/3 cup firmly packed brown sugar
1/4 cup margarine
3 bananas

1. Drain, saving 1 1/2 cups of syrup; pineapple, cherries, pears and apricots. Place in baking dish drained fruits, peaches and apples.
2. To the reserved 1 1/2 cups syrup, add lemon juice, spices and brown sugar. Pour over fruit. Dot with margarine. Bake at 250°F for 20 minutes.
4. Slice bananas and lightly stir into hot fruit. Cover, return to oven and bake for 5 minutes to heat through.

Makes about 18 servings

▤Passover Recipe

Oven: 250°F   Bake Time: 25 min.

David, age 12

Mellow Grapefruit (D or P)

Kathryn Karp

2 Tablespoons butter or margarine, melted
2 grapefruits, cut in half and sectioned
1/2 cup packed brown sugar
4 maraschino cherries
1/4 cup apricot brandy, divided usage

1. Pour melted butter over grapefruit halves.
2. Sprinkle brown sugar over each half.
3. Place cherry in center.
4. Pour 2 Tablespoons apricot brandy over grapefruit.
5. Broil about 3 minutes.
6. Pour remaining apricot brandy over grapefruit just before serving.

Makes 4 servings

▤Passover Recipe

Oven: Broil   Broil Time: 3 min.

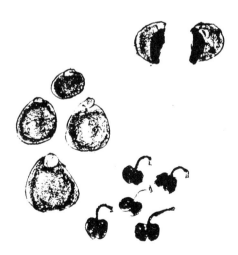

Eva, age 9

Fruit Pizza (D)

Pam Sloan

1 tube (18-20 oz.) refrigerated sugar cookie dough
1 package (8 oz.) cream cheese, softened
1/3 cup sugar
1 teaspoon vanilla
1 pint strawberries
2 banannas
2 kiwi
1 Granny Smith apple, cored
1 can (11 oz.) mandarin oranges, drained
1 small basket blueberries

1. Press cookie dough into a 14-inch circle on a pizza pan. Bake at 350°F for 10 to 15 minutes until golden brown. Remove from oven and let cool.
2. Combine cream cheese, sugar and vanilla. Spread over cooled crust.
3. Slice strawberries, bananas, kiwi and apple onto cream cheese mixture. Arrange drained mandarin oranges. Sprinkle with blueberries. Cut into wedges to serve.

Makes 8 servings

Oven: 350°F   Bake Time: 10-15 min.

Soups

Alan's Favorite Carrot Soup (D)

Alan Gertler

2 to 3 Tablespoons butter
6 to 8 large carrots, chopped
4 medium onions, chopped
2 quarts vegetable stock
2/3 cup uncooked rice
milk or cream
pepper to taste

1. Melt the butter in a large pot. Add carrots and onions. Cover and simmer over low heat for 10 to 15 minutes.
2. Add stock and rice. Bring to a boil and simmer for 25 minutes.
3. Remove from heat and puree in a blender.
4. Add milk or cream to desired consistency. Add pepper to taste.

Makes 10 to 12 servings.

Cook Time: 35 to 40 minutes

✓To prepare in advance, prepare to step 3. Don't add the milk or cream. Refrigerate. Re-heat the pureed vegetables and stock, then add the milk or cream.

✓Chicken stock may be substituted for vegetable stock but if this is done the soup is no longer a dairy dish.

✓Carrots are versatile and always available, besides they are high in vitamin A. The sweet flavor of carrrots is great in soups. If a soup or sauce needs sweetening, shred some carrots and add it to the mixture.

Mushroom Barley Soup (D)

Emmy Bell

1/2 cup raw pearl barley
8 cups stock or water
3 cloves garlic, minced
1 heaping cup (or more) chopped onion
3 tablespoons butter
1 pound mushrooms, sliced
1/4 cup tamari/soy sauce
1/4 cup dry sherry
freshly ground pepper
salt to taste

1. Cook barley in stock or water until tender, about 20 minutes.
2. While barley is cooking, sauté garlic and onion in butter until soft. Add mushrooms. Sauté.
3. To cooked barley, add mushroom mixture, tamari/soy sauce, sherry, pepper and salt to taste. Simmer 20 minutes, covered. Serve hot.

Makes 8 servings

Cook Time: 40 minutes

✓ Stock could be:

Water blended with celery and carrots.

Dried mushrooms soaked in water, then cut up and added to water for a chewy texture.

Telma® mushroom bouillon cubes (use 1 cube for each 2 cups water).

Julie's Own Veggie Soup (P)

Julie Stage

6 cups water
5-8 vegetarian bouillon cubes (chicken will do, too)
1 cup dry soup mix (containing yellow and green split
    peas, barley, alphabet noodles and no seasoning)
2 carrots, peeled and sliced on the diagonal
2 potatoes, peeled and cut into bite-sized cubes
2 zucchini, sliced
1 small onion, chopped
1 large stalk celery, sliced on the diagonal
Pepper to taste

1. Add water to a large pot. Bring to boil.
2. Add bouillon cubes and mix until dissolved, then add all
   other ingredients. Bring to boil.
3. Reduce heat and simmer about 1 hour. Serve with a tossed
   salad and bread or rolls in the Sukkah.

Makes 6 to 8 servings

Cook Time: about 1 hour

✓Potatoes come in several varieties. The four basic ones are the
LONG WHITES which are great for boiling, salads, hash
browns, home fries; ROUND REDS which are boiled whole;
ROUND WHITES which are known as chef potatoes are used
in baking, frying and salads; and the well known RUSSET
which are great for baking and frying. Other varieties are the
yellow fingerlings, Yukon gold, and purple fingerlings.

Hearty Lentil Soup (D)

Julia Rubin

2 teaspoons vegetable oil
4 large carrots, cut lengthwise in half the sliced, about 2
    cups sliced
1 bunch scallions, thinly sliced
3 cloves garlic, crushed
3 cans (10 1/2 oz. each) vegetable broth
1 cup dried lentils, rinsed and drained
1 teaspoon dried thyme
1/4 teaspoon freshly ground black pepper
1 can (10 3/4 oz.) cream of celery soup, diluted with 1
    can water
1 package (10 oz.) frozen chopped spinach
2 Tablespoons fresh lemon juice
2 cups hot cooked rice, optional

1. In a 4-quart saucepan, heat oil with carrots, scallions and
   garlic for about 5 minutes or until scallions are tender.
2. Stir in broth, lentils, thyme and pepper. Bring to boil.
   Reduce heat to low and simmer, covered for 35 minutes
   until lentils are tender.
3. Stir in cream of celery soup, water and spinach. Bring to a
   simmer and stir frequently to break up spinach. Cook only
   until spinach is completely thawed and heated through.
4. Remove from heat. Stir in lemon juice. If desired, serve
   soup over 1/2 cup rice in 4 bowls.

Makes 4 servings

Cook Time: about 40 minutes

✓Chicken stock may be substituted for vegetable stock but if
this is done the soup is no longer a dairy dish.

Bean Vegetable Soup (P)

Linda Kutten

1 bag (1 lb. 4 oz.) bean soup mix, discard seasoning
   packet
1 medium onion, chopped
3 celery stalks, chopped
2 carrots, chopped
4 tomatoes, diced
1 bunch parsley
1 lemon, juice only
3 Tablespoons Worcestershire sauce
2 cloves, garlic
1/2 teaspoon ground pepper
salt to taste
corn tortilla

1. Soak beans overnight with about 2-inches of water to cover.
2. Rinse and drain beans. Put into soup pot. Add about a quart of water. Bring to boil. Simmer for 2 hours to soften beans.
3. Add onion, celery, carrots, tomatoes, parsley leaves, lemon juice, Worcestershire sauce, garlic and pepper. Return to boil then simmer for 1 hour until vegetables are softened. Salt to taste.
4. Cut corn tortillas into strips. Scatter on baking sheet. Bake in 350°F oven for 5 to 10 minutes, or until crisp.

Makes 8 servings

Soak beans overnight.   Cook Time: 3 hours

✓Using the bag of mixed beans gives you variety without having to buy a bag of each bean. You may soak the beans ahead of time and refrigerate. Do not leave them at room temperature longer than overnight, especially during the summer months. If you see bubbles on top and the water is getting thick, you have left the beans out too long. The bacteria population has taken over and is enjoying the beans.

SOUPS

Kreplach with Beef Filling (M)

Shirley Rutkovitz

Dough
1 egg
1/4 cup water
pinch salt
1 Tablespoon vegetable oil
1 1/2 cups flour

Filling
1 onion, chopped
1 Tablespoon vegetable oil
about 6 ounces cooked, trimmed chuck steak
2 hard cooked eggs
salt and pepper to taste
chicken fat, if desired

1. Mix together ingredients for dough. Knead to a smooth ball. Divide into 2 balls. Cover and let rest.
2. Sauté onion in oil until soft. Then grind in food processor or food grinder with cooked meat and eggs. Mix in salt and pepper to taste and chicken fat as needed to moisten.
3. Roll each ball of dough thin to about 9-inch square. Cut into 3-inch circles.
4. Put a rounded 1/2 teaspoon of filling in center of each circle. Bring edge over to make a half circle. Seal edges with fork. If needed, wet edges with water to seal.
5. Cook in boiling water for 10 to 15 minutes. Put only half of the kreplachs in the pot at a time. Take out with a slotted spoon. Serve in chicken soup.

Makes 36 kreplachs

Cook Time: 10-15 min.

KREPLACH is a noodle dough filled with various fillings. Similar to boiled wontons, tortellini, etc. It is usually served in a soup but it can be served with a sauce or pan-fried.

Kreplach with Chicken Filling (M)

Julie Stage

Chicken Filling
2-3 large chicken breasts
1/2 small onion
salt & pepper to taste

Noodle Dough
2 eggs
1 Tablespoon cold water
1 1/3 cups flour
1/2 teaspoon salt
cooking pot
boiling water or chicken soup

1. *Filling*: Cook chicken breasts in a small amount of water. Save broth. Grind cooked chicken and raw onion together in food processor. Season to taste. If needed, add a slight amount of broth to keep the mixture slightly moist.
2. *For dough*: Combine all noodle dough ingredients. Mix and knead well until elastic. On lightly floured surface, roll dough as thin as possible into a rectangle (Do not use too much flour on the surface as it will make the dough stiff.) Cut into 3-inch squares.
3. Place about a rounded teaspoonful of filling on half of square, toward one corner. Fold other half over filling to form a triangle. With wet fingers, press edges firmly together. Seal.
4. Drop kreplach in boiling water or chicken soup. Cover and cook 15-20 minutes until tender. Serve hot.

Makes about 30 kreplachs.

Cook Time: 15-20 min.

✍ This recipe is from my maternal grandmother, Dora Bolker. Traditionally, my family ate Kreplach in chicken soup for Rosh Hashanah.

SOUPS

Dill Chicken Soup (M)

Adrienne Tropp

1 large chicken, cut into eighths (or 4 chicken breasts)
3 1/2 quarts water
2 onions, quartered
1/2 Tablespoon salt
2 carrots
3 stalks celery
1 Tablespoon parsley or to taste
1 Tablespoon dill weed or to taste

1. Place chicken in large pot with water and onions. Bring to boil. Lower heat to medium, cook for 1 1/2 hours.
2. Add remaining ingredients. Cover and cook over low heat 1 hour or longer.
3. Remove chicken and strain soup. Let soup cool, then skim off fat. Remove chicken meat from bones and save.
4. To serve: Heat soup. Add vegetables of your choice and some of the cooked chicken meat or leave as a clear broth.

Makes 8 servings

Cook Time: 2 1/2 hours

▤Passover Recipe

✓Some of the cooked chicken can go into the soup. Some can be sprinkled with paprika and heated in the oven for another meal. I usually use the breast meat to make a dill chicken salad: cut up the chicken, add finely chopped onion, dill and mayonnaise to taste. Let stand 4 hours for best flavor.

▤CHICKEN SOUP. We had a difficult time getting a chicken soup recipe. Many cooks just know what to put into the soup without a recipe. Then they adjust the seasonings as their mother or grandmother would do. We finally got two recipes to get you started. Dill is the traditional flavoring. You personalize the broth with the herbs and spices you like.

SOUPS

Pam's Chicken Soup (M)

Pam Sloan

1 whole (4 to 5 pound) chicken
2 large onions, peeled, quartered
1 large parsnip, 1-inch slices
2 stalks celery, chunks
2 carrots, chunks
1 bunch parsley
3 quarts water
salt and pepper to taste

To Serve
baby carrots or vegetable you like
matzo balls, rice or egg noodles

1. Place first seven ingredients in stock pot. Water should cover all. Bring to boil then simmer for 1 1/2 hours with cover askew until chicken is cooked and tender. If not, cook for another 30 minutes.
2. Remove just breast and thigh meat from chicken, cut in bite size pieces and refrigerate. Leave rest in pot and continue simmering for 1 1/2 hours.
3. Strain chicken and vegetables from soup. The easiest method is to sit a colander in a large bowl or pot that will collect the soup, line colander with cheesecloth, then dump the whole pot of soup onto the cheese cloth. Lift the colander to drain. Sit the colander on a plate to catch remaining soup. Gather edges of cheesecloth to bag vegetables and chicken and toss as the flavor will have been cooked out of them.
4. Cool soup. Skim fat from top of soup. (Refrigerate the soup overnight to congeal the fat which will just lift off.)
5. An hour before serving, heat soup to boiling. Add chicken meat and baby carrots. Simmer to cook carrots, about 30 minutes. Serve soup with matzo balls, rice or egg noodles.

Makes about 2 1/2 quarts soup   Cook Time: 3 1/2 hours

SOUPS

Matzo Balls (P or M)

Sharon Honig-Bear

2 Tablespoons vegetable oil or margarine
2 large eggs, slightly beaten
1/2 cup matzo meal
1 teaspoon salt
2 Tablespoons soup stock or water

1. Beat together oil and eggs. Add matzo meal and salt. Blend well.
2. Add soup stock and mix until uniform and thick.
3. Cover mixing bowl and place in refrigerator for at least 15 minutes.
4. Using a big pot, bring at least two quarts of water to a boil. Reduce flame and drop balls approximately 1-inch in diameter in the water. Keep hands wet for ease in forming the balls.
5. Cover pot and cook for 30-40 minutes.

Makes 8 to 10 balls

Sitting Time: at least 15 min.   Cook Time: 40 min.

▤Passover Recipe

✍I grew up in a family that loved hard matzo balls— the more like golf balls, the better. Ironically, people often ask me how I get my matzo balls so light. My recipe comes right off the box of matzo meal! The key is making the mixture the night before or early on the day you plan to cook them.

✓ For a fluffier ball, refrigerate batter for 6-12 hours. Balls will grow in size by 3-4 times. Place the balls in chicken soup when they are finished for more taste. This recipe doubles, triples, even quadruples easily. I always reduce the salt considerably.

SOUPS

Chicken-Avocado Tortilla Soup (M)

Adrienne Tropp

1/3 cup chopped onion
3 cloves garlic, chopped
3/4 teaspoon ground cumin
3/4 teaspoon dried oregano
1/4 teaspoon chili powder
1/4 teaspoon pepper
8 cups defatted chicken broth (I use prepared broth in cartons)
1 can (14 oz.) diced tomatoes
1 can (4 oz.) diced green chilies
10 corn tortillas (6-inch diameter)
1 1/2 pounds boneless, skinned chicken breasts
1 firm-ripe avocado, peeled, pitted and thinly sliced
2 Tablespoons chopped fresh cilantro

1. In a 5 to 6 quart pot over medium heat, stir onion, garlic, cumin, oregano, chili powder and pepper until spices are fragrant, about 1 minute.
2. Add broth, tomatoes (including juices), and green chilies. Cover and bring to a boil over high heat.
3. Meanwhile, stack tortillas and cut into 1/8-inch wide strips. Add to boiling broth. Reduce heat, cover, and simmer for 15 minutes, stirring occasionally. The tortillas will thicken the soup as they dissolve.
4. Rinse chicken and cut into 1/2-inch pieces. Add to broth and return to a boil over high heat. Reduce heat, cover and simmer until chicken is white in the center (cut to test), about 5 minutes.
5. To serve: ladle soup into bowls, garnish with avocado and cilantro.

Makes 6 servings

Cook Time: about 30 min.

Passover Recipe   Quick & Easy Meal

Cabbage Borscht (M)

Debbie Pomeranz

About 1 1/2 to 2 pounds short ribs or small pot roast
soup bone with marrow
water
salt to taste
1 large onion, chopped
l large can (28 oz.) stewed tomatoes
2 Tablespoons brown sugar
1/2 teaspoon sour salt (citric acid)
1/2 head and 1/2 head shredded cabbage

1. Place meat and soup bone in large pot. Cover with water.
   Salt to your taste. Boil. Skim until clear. Cover and
   simmer 1 hour.
2. Add onion, tomatoes, sugar, sour salt and 1/2 head
   shredded cabbage. Cook 2 hours.
3. Add remaining 1/2 head shredded cabbage and cook for 1/2
   hour more.
4. Adjust taste for sweet/sour flavor.

Makes about 8 servings

Cook Time: 3 1/2 hours

▤Passover Recipe

▤BORSCHT is a sour Russian soup with many variations.
Many know it best as a cold beet soup served with a dollop of
sour cream, but it can be made from any vegetable and
includes many vegetables.

Short Ribs And Cabbage Soup (M)

Emmy Bell

Beef short ribs, 1-2 pieces per person
2 quarts water
2 onions, diced
1 to 2 cans (16 oz. each) cut-up tomatoes with juice
1 head cabbage, coarsely shredded
1 teaspoon salt
1/2 teaspoon pepper
1/4 cup lemon juice
1 tablespoon packed brown sugar
1 cup raisins

1. Boil short ribs in water, skimming frequently.
2. Add onions and tomatoes. Cover pot. Cook over low heat for 1 hour.
3. Add cabbage, salt, and pepper. Cover and cook another hour.
4. Add lemon juice, brown sugar and raisins. Cook 20 minutes more.

Makes 8 to 10 servings

Cook Time: 2 1/2 hours

▤Passover Recipe

✍This recipe is from Rose Luterman who never wrote down a recipe in her life. I took notes as she cooked.

Sweet and Sour Cabbage Soup (M)

Helene Paris

12 cups water
1 1/2 to 2 pounds short ribs (flanken if you can get it)
1 head cabbage (about 2-3 pounds) cut in strips or 1-
    inch squares
1 large onion, chopped
1 cup ketchup
1 can (28 oz.) whole peeled tomatoes, chopped into
    pieces
1/2 cup sugar
1/3 cup fresh lemon juice
2 Tablespoons sweet paprika
1 Tablespoon salt or more to taste

1. Add water and short ribs to stainless steel or enameled
   kettle. Bring to boil, skimming froth as it rises. Simmer 1
   hour.
2. Remove meat, trim fat and discard bones. Cut meat into
   tiny pieces. Skim fat off broth.
3. Add to defatted broth, meat and remaining ingredients.
   Simmer for 30 minutes. Adjust seasoning to taste with
   lemon juice, salt or sugar.

Makes 8 servings

Cook Time: 1 1/2 hours

✓The soup improves with age. It is best made a couple of days
ahead. Cool the soup so it's not steaming then refrigerate in a
shallow pan or bowl. You want to quickly chill the soup and yet
not overwork your refrigerator. If the pan is deep, it would take
a long time for the center to cool, allowing the bacteria
population to grow and spoil your efforts.

✓I prefer the cabbage cut into 1-inch squares instead of strips.

SALADS

Hummus (P)

Jewish Fest Recipe

3 cloves garlic
2 cans (15 oz. each) garbanzo beans
1/4 teaspoon red chili pepper
1/4 teaspoon cumin
1/2 cup tahini (sesame purée)
1/4 cup lemon juice
1/2 teaspoon salt
pita wedges

1. In food processor chop garlic.
2. Add drained garbanzo, saving liquid. Blend until smooth. Add 1/4 cup bean liquid to begin thinning.
3. Add remaining ingredients. Blend. Add more bean liquid to reach desired consistency. Chill
4. Serve with pita wedges on a lettuce leaf as a salad or as an appetizer.

Makes about 4 cups

✓Garbanzo beans are also called chick peas or chi-chi beans. The canned beans make it easy to make the hummus. Ground dried beans are used to make falafel.

Tabbouleh (P)

Nancy Simkin, Jewish Fest Recipe

1 cup (5.25 oz.) medium grain bulgur
cold water to cover
1 1/2 cup minced parsley
1/2 cup minced mint
1 bunch green onions, finely chopped
1 small cucumber, peeled, seeded and diced
1/2 cup lemon juice
3/4 cup olive oil
2 cloves garlic, pressed
1/2 teaspoon cumin
1/4 teaspoon salt
1/4 teaspoon pepper
3 tomatoes, seeded and diced

1. Cover bulgur with cold water and let rehydrate for 1 hour.
2. Drain bulgur. Squeeze dry, getting as much of the water out as possible.
3. Toss bulgur with parsley, mint, green onions, and cucumber.
4. Shake together in a jar the lemon juice, olive oil, garlic, cumin, salt, and pepper.
5. Pour lemon juice mixture over bulgur. Toss to mix in well. Chill.
6. Just before serving, mix in tomatoes. Serve with pita wedges.

Makes 7 cups

Couscous with Apricots (P)

Janice Saks

1 box (10 oz.) couscous
1/2 cup water
1 cup orange juice
olive oil
2 Tablespoons white wine vinegar
8 dried apricots, thinly sliced
1 Tablespoon dried currants
1 Tablespoon golden raisins
2 teaspoons grated fresh ginger
1/4 medium red onion, finely diced
2 Tablespoons white wine vinegar
2 Tablespoons toasted pine nuts

1. Pour couscous into small mixing bowl.
2. In saucepan, combine water, orange juice, olive oil, and 2 Tablespoons vinegar in saucepan. Bring to a boil and stir in dried fruits and ginger. Pour immediately over couscous. Cover bowl and let stand for 20 minutes.
3. Bring a small pot of water to a boil and drop in red onions for 15 seconds. Drain well and toss onions with 2 Tablespoons vinegar to retain color.
4. Fluff couscous with fork and add pine nuts and onions. Toss and serve.

Makes about 8 servings

Stand Time: 20 min.

✓Couscous is a North African pasta, semolina. Most of the couscous we see in the local stores are shaped like tiny beads but they do come in larger sizes. The tiny pasta cooks very quickly.

Mother's Macaroni Salad (P)

Shirley Rutkovitz

1 package (1 pound) small elbow macaroni
1 jar (10 oz.) green olives stuffed with pimientos
8 or 10 eggs, hard cooked
3 to 4 stalks celery, sliced
Mayonnaise
Paprika

1. Cook macaroni in boiling water. Drain and cool.
2. Drain and slice olives.
3. Chop, not too finely, 8 eggs. Slice the remaining 2 eggs and reserve for garnishing top of salad.
4. Combine olives, eggs and celery with enough mayonnaise to hold together. Add a couple shakes of paprika for color.
5. Mix cooled macaroni with egg mixture. Add more mayonnaise if desired. Place in serving dish. Garnish with sliced egg and sprinkle paprika over top for color.

Makes about 8 servings

Cooked Vegetable Macaroni Salad (P)

Elizabeth Kempler

1 cup elbow macaroni, cooked
1 cup diced carrots, cooked
1 cup frozen green peas, cooked
1 cup diced beets, cooked
1 cup cauliflower, cooked
1 cup French dressing
salt to taste
lettuce leaves, tomatoes, black olives

1. Combine macaroni, carrots, peas, beets and cauliflower.
2. Add dressing and salt.
3. Spoon onto lettuce leaves and garnish with sliced tomatoes and black olives.

Makes 6-8 servings

Tortellini Salad With Pesto (D)

Rabbi Myra Soifer

Pesto
1 cup, moderately well-packed basil leaves, rinsed and
    dried well
1/3 cup olive oil
2 cloves garlic, chopped
1/4 cup grated Parmesan cheese
1 Tablespoon unsalted butter, softened

Pasta
1 pound fresh or frozen tortellini (choose your favorite
    kind; the small ones work best)
1 Tablespoon pine nuts.

1. For the pesto, combine the basil, olive oil, garlic, cheese, and butter in a blender or food processor.
2. For the pasta, boil according to directions, until tender but not mushy. Drain thoroughly, then place in a serving bowl.
3. Stir the pesto into the pasta. Sprinkle on the pine nuts. You can use a few extra sprigs of basil as garnish, if you like.

Makes about 4 servings

✍On my 1998 sabbatical in Berkeley, California, I discovered a community of vegetarian Jews, many were shomer shabbas (Sabbath observant) and won't cook on Shabbat. It was a challenge for me, a person seriously disinclined toward vegetables, to find Sabbath potluck dish that I would enjoy. This Tortellini Salad did the trick.

✓ It is best served at room temperature. It can be made in advance and "keeps" very well. For best results, keep the pesto separate from the pasta until just prior to serving. Also, the pesto sauce is very good. Make some up and store it in ice cube trays in the freezer. Pop out a "cube" for serving on any sort of pasta.

New York Style Potato Salad (P)

Adrienne Tropp

6 cups diced, cooked potatoes
1 1/2 cups sliced celery
1/2 cup cut-up scallions
1/4 cup sliced radishes
2 Tablespoons snipped parsley
1 cup mayonnaise
1 Tablespoon vinegar
2 teaspoons prepared mustard
1/2 teaspoon celery seeds
1 1/2 to 2 teaspoons salt
1/8 teaspoon pepper

1. Toss together all ingredients.
2. Cover and refrigerate for several hours for the flavors to meld.

Makes 6 servings

Refrigerate: Several hours to meld flavors

☰Passover Recipe

✓Store potatoes in a dry dark place.

✓Try putting an apple with the potatoes to prevent budding.

✓Storing the potatoes in the refrigerator may cause the starch to turn to sugar, making a very sweet potato. Potato chip makers know the importance of controlling the storage temperature of potatoes. If too much sugar is produced, the chip will burn quickly.

Bok Choy Salad (P)

Helene Paris

2 packages (3 oz. each) ramen noodle soup
1/2 cup sunflower seeds
3 Tablespoons slivered almonds, chopped
1/2 cup sugar
1/4 cup olive oil
1/4 cup cider vinegar
2 Tablespoons soy sauce
1 head bok choy, shredded
6 green onions, chopped

1. Remove flavor packets from soup mix, reserve for another use. Crumble noodles.
2. Combine noodles, sunflower seeds and almonds. Spread on a 15x10-inch jellyroll pan. Bake at 350°F for 8 to10 minutes or until golden brown. Set aside.
3. In a saucepan over medium heat, bring sugar, olive oil, vinegar and soy sauce to a boil. Remove from heat and cool.
4. In a large bowl, place bok choy and green onions. Drizzle with sugar mixture. Add ramen mixture and toss well.

Makes 6 to 8 servings

Oven 350°F   Bake Time: 10 min.

Broccoli Slaw (M)

Helene Paris

2 packages (3 oz. each) ramen oriental flavor noodle
    soup
1 package (16 oz.) broccoli slaw
1/2 bunch green onions, cut into small pieces
1/2 cup vegetable oil
2/3 cup white vinegar
3/4 cup sugar
3 ounces toasted slivered almonds
4 ounces toasted sunflower seeds (comes in a jar)

1. Break noodles into pieces by placing in a plastic bag and
    pounding gently with a mallet works well.
2. Mix noodles, slaw, and green onions.
3. Wisk together oil, vinegar, sugar and 1 seasoning packet.
    Pour over slaw mixture. Refrigerate overnight. Stir a
    couple of times during refrigeration.
4. Before serving, add toasted almonds and sunflower seeds.

Makes 6 to 8 servings

Refrigerate Time: Overnight

✓Broccoli has tight compact bud clusters on stems. The
broccoli slaw is made from the stems. The stems are shredded
then bagged, ready-to-use.

SALADS

Mediterranean Salad (P)

Helene Paris, Jewish Fest Recipe

1 bag (10 oz.) Romaine salad
1 bag (12 oz.) American Salad
2 medium tomatoes, diced
1 cucumber, quartered lengthwise and sliced
1 red onion, sliced
6 ounces feta cheese, crumbled
3 ounces pitted Kalamata olives

Dressing
1/4 cup white vinegar
1/4 cup lemon juice
1/4 cup olive oil
1 teaspoon oregano
1/2 teaspoon salt

1. Toss all ingredients together just before serving.
2. Serve with pita wedges.

Makes 12 cups, 12 servings 1 cup each.

▤Passover Recipe

✓The American salad contains iceberg, romaine, carrots, red cabbage, and radishes.

✓Do not toss the dressing into the vegetables until ready to serve. The lettuce wilts quickly. Just have all the salad ingredients in the bowl. Place a wet paper towel over. Cover with plastic wrap and refrigerate. Then just before serving toss in the salad dressing.

✓Be sure to get pitted Kalamata olives.

Camille's Favorite Salad (P)

Camille Gertler

1 pound asparagus
handful of pecans (about 1/4 cup)
basket of strawberries (1 pint)
1 bag (5 oz.) mixed baby greens
raspberry vinaigrette

1. Boil the asparagus and cut into 1-inch sections, discarding ends. Let cool.
2. Roast pecans and allow to cool.
3. Clean and trim strawberries.
4. Toss together asparagus, pecans, strawberries and greens. Add raspberry vinaigrette to taste.

Makes 6 to 8 servings   ▤Passover Recipe

Cucumber Salad (P)

Helene Paris, Jewish Fest Recipe

1/4 teaspoon and 1 teaspoon salt
3 large cucumbers, peeled and thinly sliced
1 large onion, thinly sliced
1/2 cup vinegar
2 Tablespoons cold water
2 teaspoons sugar
1/8 teaspoon pepper
1/8 teaspoon dried tarragon
1/8 teaspoon dried basil

1. Sprinkle 1/4 teaspoon salt over cucumbers. Let sit two minutes.
2. Drain cucumbers. Add all remaining ingredients and 1 teaspoon salt. Chill.

Makes 8 servings   ▤Passover Recipe

Shelly's Orange-Poppy Salad (P)

Janice Saks

Dressing
1/2 teaspoon sugar
dash of pepper
2 Tablespoons poppy seeds
2 Tablespoons balsamic vinegar
3 Tablespoons olive oil

Salad:
1 can (10 oz.) mandarin oranges, drained
1 avocado, chopped
1 medium red onion, chopped
2 heads red leaf lettuce

1. At least 12 hours in advance, mix dressing ingredients in a covered jar and shake well.
2. Toss together all ingredients immediately before serving.

Makes about 8 servings

▤Passover Recipe

✓Poppy seeds look like round beads, but if you looked at the poppy seed under a magnifying glass you'll see that they are kidney shaped.

✓The term mandarin oranges is used for clementines, satsuma, tangerines, temple orange, among some others.

Holiday Gelatin Salad (D)

Barbara Pratt

3 packages (3 oz. each) strawberry flavored gelatin
    (regular or sugar-free)
3 cups boiling water
1 package (10 oz.) frozen sliced or diced strawberries
2 bananas, mashed
1 can (8 oz.) crushed pineapple, drained
1 carton (8 oz.) sour cream

1. Dissolve gelatin in boiling water stirring for at least 2 minutes.
2. Stir in frozen strawberries until thawed.
3. Add bananas and pineapple. Pour half of the mixture into a shallow 2-quart dish. Freeze for 30 minutes or just until set. Keep remaining mixture at room temperature, stirring occasionally to prevent it from setting.
4. Spread sour cream on top of soft frozen gelatin in pan. Then carefully pour remaining gelatin mixture over all. Refrigerate 3 hours or longer until set. Cut into squares and serve.

Makes about 8 servings

Freeze: 30 minutes then Refrigerate at least 3 hours

▤Pasover Recipe

✐This recipe is a favorite of my family at holiday dinners. My mother's late cousin, Shirley Kazen made it. Eventually, it became a tradition for any special celebration or holiday meal.

BEEF

Wendy's Brisket (M)

Wendy Alderman

4 pounds beef brisket
1 can (6 oz.) tomato paste
1 envelope (1.4 oz.) dried onion soup mix
1 can beer or 1 1/2 cups wine
onion, potato, carrots

1. Place all ingredients except vegetables in covered roasting or baking pan. Bake at 350°F for about 2 hours.
2. Uncover and add cut up vegetables to taste. Replace cover and cook about another hour. Slice meat and serve.

Oven: 350°F   Bake Time: 3 hours

✓ Oven bags make clean up even easier.

✓ In place of beer, use wine for Passover.

BRISKET is a tradition for Sabbath, Hanukkah, and family events. It can be prepared in many ways. Temple Sinai Brisket Cook Off of 2002 had thirteen entries—no two were alike!

✓ Remember about half of the weight of the beginning piece of brisket will be trimmed as fat or cooked away. A 5-pound piece of brisket will cook down to about 2 1/2 pounds of meat. So calculate about eight (5-ounce) servings from a 5-pound brisket. But you'll have to judge your family's appetite.

✓ Most cooks like to cook the brisket the day before, refrigerate, take off the congealed fat, slice and reheat.

Mrs. Teitelbaum's Brisket (M)

Rabbi Myra Soifer

Nice cut of brisket of beef, approximately 3-5 pounds
1 to 2 envelopes (1.4 oz. each) dried onion soup mix
Heavy-duty aluminum foil

1. Preheat oven to 325°F.
2. Pat dry soup mix onto the brisket. Use 1 or 2 envelopes, depending on size of the brisket.
3. Wrap tightly in heavy-duty aluminum foil.
4. Bake at 325°F for approximately 3 1/2 hours.

Oven: 325°F   Bake Time: 3 1/2 hours

✍Barry Teitelbaum was a friend from my first congregation in New Orleans. I never met his mom, but he passed along her never-fail brisket recipe to me.

✓The longer and slower you bake this, the better it will taste. But be sure that the brisket is tightly wrapped in the foil, since the "secret" to delicious brisket is the juices from the soup. You don't want those juices to "escape"!

✓Whatever you do, don't salt the brisket. The onion soup is salty enough. This is not a recipe for those watching their fat!!

BEEF

Newman's Deli Brisket (M)

Karen Newman

5 pounds brisket or more

Per 5 pounds of brisket:
2 envelopes (1.4 oz. each) dried onion soup mix
2 cans beer

1. Place brisket in pan.
2. Put soup mix on top of brisket.
3. Pour beer around sides and a little on top.
4. Bake at 325°F, covered with tight foil wrap, for 3 hours or until tender.

Oven: 325°F   Bake Time: 3 hours or till tender

Chili Sauce Brisket (M)

Linda Kutten

5-pound brisket, remove all visible fat
salt and pepper
1 large onion, chopped
1/2 cup water
1 bottle (12 oz.) chili sauce
1/4 cup parsley

1. Wash and dry brisket. Salt and pepper to taste.
2. Place onion and water in bottom of heavy deep roasting pan. Put brisket on top. Pour chili sauce over brisket and sprinkle with parsley.
3. Bake, covered, at 325°F for 4 to 5 hours or until fork tender.

Oven: 325°F   Bake Time: 4-5 hours

✓ I like to trim as much fat off as I can. I have found no difference in tenderness or flavor whether the fat is left on or trimmed completely as there still is a lot of fat in the meat.

Savory Brisket (M)

Linda Kutten

5-6 pound brisket
6 cloves garlic, crushed
2 large onions, chopped
6 carrots, chopped
4 stalks celery, chopped
1 can (8 oz.) tomato sauce
1 envelope (1.4 oz.) dried onion soup

1. Trim fat from brisket. Rinse with water. Pat dry. Rub all over with garlic. Place brisket in baking pan.
2. Add to baking pan, onions, carrots and celery. Pour tomato sauce over all. Sprinkle onion soup on top.
3. Cover and bake at 325°F for 3 hours.
4. Remove cover and bake 30 minutes more.

Oven: 325°F   Bake Time: 3 hrs. 30 min.

✓The brisket is better if prepared a day ahead. Remove brisket from pan, wrap tightly and refrigerate. Pour the juices into a bowl, cover and refrigerate. Once the fat has solidified, discard fat. Slice brisket, pour cooking liquid over brisket and reheat, covered in 350°F oven for 30 minutes or until hot.

✓Brisket is beef from the breast section under the first 5 ribs. It may be sold in two sections: FLAT CUT has less fat and may be more expensive and the POINT which has more fat and more flavor.

Mom's Brisket (M)

Nancy Daum

3 large onions, sliced
bay leaves
1 large brisket of beef
seasonings and herbs from your kitchen
2 bottles (12 oz. each) chili sauce

BEEF

1. Place sliced onions in roasting dish.
2. Put 1 bay leaf on top of onions then put brisket on top of all, fat side up. Put another bay leaf on top of brisket.
3. Sprinkle on top with all the seasonings and herbs you have. I season with salt, pepper, onion powder, celery salt, garlic powder, marjoram, thyme, oregano, cumin, chili powder, and cloves.
4. Spread 2 bottles of chili sauce thickly over the seasoned brisket. Swish water into chili bottles to rinse. Add 1-2 bottles of water to pan, depending on size of brisket. Do not cover.
5. Bake at 250°F (electric) or 275°F (gas) for 6 hours. Don't panic-the top gets black.

Oven: 250°F(electric), 275°F (gas)   Bake Time: 6 hours

✓For the seasonings and herbs use your judgment and your personal preferences.

Barbecued Brisket (M)

Linda Kutten

5 pound brisket
1 Tablespoon liquid smoke
1 medium onion, chopped
1 clove garlic, peeled and halved
salt and pepper to taste
3 Tablespoons brown sugar
1 bottle (16 oz.) ketchup
1/2 cup water
2 Tablespoons Worcestershire sauce
1 Tablespoon dry mustard

1. Trim fat, wash and dry brisket. Rub liquid smoke over all. Place in baking pan with onions and garlic. Salt and pepper. Cover. Bake at 325°F for 5 hours.
2. Meanwhile, combine brown sugar, ketchup, water, Worcestershire sauce and mustard. Set aside.
3. Remove cooked brisket. Thinly slice. Pour sauce over slices. Cover. Bake at 350°F for 30 minutes until heated through and bubbly.

Oven: 325°F & 350°F   Bake Time: 5 hrs. 30 min.

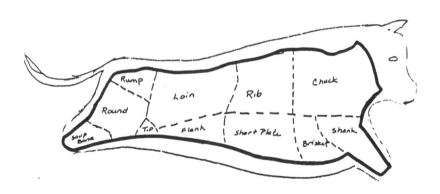

Lynne's BBQ Brisket (M)

Lynne Daus

5 pound brisket
2 medium onions, chopped
1 1/2 cups water
2 cups ketchup
4 Tablespoons brown sugar
4 Tablespoons vinegar
1/2 cup lemon juice
3 to 4 Tablespoons Worcestershire sauce
3 teaspoons dry mustard
dash of cayenne pepper

BEEF

1. Bake brisket, covered, at 275°F for 3 hours.
2. Remove brisket from pan. Remove fat from drippings. Return brisket to baking pan with skimmed drippings.
3. Sauté onion in large skillet. Add water, ketchup, brown sugar, vinegar, lemon juice, Worcestershire sauce, mustard and cayenne.
4. Pour sauce over brisket in pan. Bake at 350°F for 1 hour more.

Oven: 275°F & 350°F   Bake Time: 4 hours

Grandmother's Brisket (M)

Marilyn Kurzman

1 flat cut brisket (5 to 6 pounds)
garlic powder, onion powder, salt, pepper, paprika
1 yellow onion, sliced
2 cups ketchup
1 cup burgundy wine
1 cup water
1 envelope (1.4 oz.) dried onion soup mix
1 can (6 oz.) mushroom steak sauce
carrots
white rose potatoes, quartered

1. Trim excess fat from brisket. Sprinkle all over with garlic powder, onion powder, salt, pepper, and paprika. Place onion slices in bottom of roasting pan. Place brisket on top of onions. Mix together ketchup, wine and water. Pour half of mixture over brisket. Sprinkle onion soup mix on top. Bake uncovered at 350°F for 45 minutes.
3. Baste brisket with cooking liquid in pan, cover, bake 45 minutes.
4. Mix remaining ketchup mixture with steak sauce and pour over brisket. Bake uncovered for 30 minutes.
5.   Place carrots and potatoes around brisket. Add water to cover vegetables, baste brisket, cover and bake for 1 1/2 hours or until brisket is fork tender and potatoes are brown.
6. Let rest 15 minutes. Slice brisket thin with an electric knife and serve. (Best if refrigerated overnight to remove hardened fat. Slice and reheat covered in 250°F oven for 45 minutes.)

Oven: 350°F   Bake Time: 3 1/2 hours

✓My maternal grandmother used lima beans for vegetables. I use Dawn Fresh® Mushroom Steak Sauce.

Pineapple Brisket (M)

Adrienne Tropp

5 pound brisket
water

Glaze
4 slices pineapple
6 Tablespoons honey
1/2 cup pineapple juice
4 Tablespoons sugar

BEEF

1. Place brisket in roasting pan. Add water to 1/2-inch deep. Cover. Bake at 325°F for 2 1/2 hours.
2. Remove brisket from pan. Remove fat from drippings. Return brisket to baking pan. Place pineapple slices on top of brisket.
3. In a saucepan, combine honey, pineapple juice and sugar. Bring to boil. Pour over brisket and pineapple slices.
4. Return brisket to oven and bake at 425°F for 35 minutes.

Oven: 325°F & 425°F　　　Bake Time: 2 1/2 hrs & 35 min.

▤Passover Recipe

✓Pineapple is a native of northern South America. The fruit is so named because it looks like a pine cone. At one time Hawaii produced most of the canned pineapples; now it cans a miniscule amount. The cayenne pineapple was developed and grown in Hawaii to fit the can.

Stove-Top Brisket (M)

Linda Duffié

2 onions, quartered
about 5 pound brisket
freshly ground pepper
2 cloves garlic, minced
paprika
1 envelope (1.4 oz.) dried onion or onion-mushroom
    soup mix
1 cup red wine or beef broth
water
4 to 8 mushrooms, quartered
2 to 4 carrots, cut-up
5 to 8 small potatoes, quartered

To Thicken Pan Juices, if desired
1 Tablespoon cornstarch
2 Tablespoons water

1. In a large, deep skillet layer onions. Place brisket on top.
    Season with pepper, garlic, paprika and soup mix.
2. Bring to slow boil. Turn heat down to low. Simmer,
    covered, for 2 hours.
3. Add mushrooms, carrots and potatoes. Cover. Cook until
    brisket is tender, about 1 hour.
4. Remove brisket from pot. Slice across the grain. Place on
    serving plate. Put vegetables around brisket. Keep warm.
5. Skim fat off pan juices and serve with brisket. If you prefer
    a thick gravy, mix cornstarch and water and stir into
    boiling pan juices. Boil and stir till thickened.

Simmer 3 hours

✓This is my mother's, Patricia Duffié, recipe. The ingredients
are given with a range of amounts. Use the amount that you
feel your family would want.

BEEF

7-bone Roast (M)

Linda Duffié

about 3 pounds chuck or 7-bone roast
2 to 4 Tablespoon low salt soy sauce
2 to 3 Tablespoon ground ginger
freshly ground pepper to taste

1. Pierce roast liberally with fork.
2. Pour soy sauce over both sides. Sprinkle all over with ginger and press into meat until it is pasty. Cover. Refrigerate and let marinate for 2 to 3 hours or overnight
3. The roast may be grilled on the barbecue grill or in a pan on the stovetop. First, bring the roast to room temperature, then cook.
4. *If cooking on the stovetop*, place in oiled, heated skillet. Cover. Cook for about 1 hour or more, depending on the size and thickness of the roast and on the doneness desired. Be sure to turn roast a few times while cooking. Add freshly ground pepper for more heat.
5. *If cooking on a barbecue grill*, consult your grill cookbook to cook by indirect heat.

Makes 4 to 5 servings

Marinate: 2-3 hours or overnight   Cook Time: 1 hour

✓Chuck roast is a 7-bone roast. The blade bone that connects to the shoulder looks like a "7" when cut. There will be some waste as the meat nearest the bone often does not get as tender as the rest. I use the meat and bones to start beef soup.

✓The amount of soy sauce and ginger depends on your taste. Start with the lower amount and increase the next time you make it, if it needed more seasonings.

BEEF

Tsimmes with Short Ribs (M)

Beatrice N. Brown

3 sweet potatoes, peeled, cut in chunks
2 white potatoes, peeled, cut in chunks
1 1/2 pounds carrots, peeled, cut in thin rounds
little grated onion
1 Tablespoon packed brown sugar
salt and pepper to taste
little water
1/2 to 1 pound beef short ribs
1 cup prunes

1. In a large casserole, mix together all ingredients except beef short ribs and prunes .
2. Place short ribs on top of vegetables. Cover and cook slowly for 2 hours.
3. Add prunes. Add more water, if necessary. Cover and cook for 1 to 2 more hours.

Makes about 6 servings

Cook Time: 3-4 hours

▤Passover Recipe

▤TSIMMES means fuss or excitement in Yiddish. In cooking it is a sweet stew of vegetables, fruits and possibly meat. The vegetable, usually carrots, is cut in rounds to resemble coins. Below is a recipe with vegetables and meat. In the vegetable section of the book there is a recipe for "Tsimmes for Rosh Hashanah" with no meat but is has carrots and fruit.

Moo Shu Beef (M)

Adrienne Tropp

1 pound beef round, cut in thin strips
2 Tablespoons reduced-sodium soy sauce
1 Tablespoon dark sesame oil
2 cloves garlic, crushed
2 teaspoons sugar
3 cups packaged coleslaw mix
2/3 cup sliced green onions
1 Tablespoon cornstarch
1/4 cup water
8 medium flour tortillas, warmed
1/3 cup hoisin sauce

1. In bowl combine beef slices, soy sauce, 2 tablespoons water, sesame oil, garlic and sugar. Cover and marinate in refrigerator 20 minutes.
2. Heat large nonstick skillet over medium-high heat until hot. Add half of the beef strips. Stir-fry 1 to 2 minutes or until outside surface is no longer pink. Do not overcook. Remove from pan and cook remaining beef strips.
3. Return cooked beef strips to pan. Add coleslaw mix, green onions and cornstarch mixed with 1/4 cup water. Cook and stir until sauce is thickened and bubbly.
4. To serve: spread one side of tortilla with 2 teaspoons hoisin sauce. Spoon about 1/2 cup of beef mixture in center. Fold bottom edge up over filling. Fold sides to center, overlapping edges.

Makes 4 servings

Marinate: 20 min.   Cook Time: about 5 min.

⌛Quick & Easy Meal

BEEF

Sweet and Sour Meatballs (M)

Pat Kay

3 pounds ground beef
3 eggs, beaten
1 grated potato or breadcrumbs
vegetable oil
2 bottles (12 oz. each) chili sauce
1 large jar (12 oz.) grape jelly or less to taste
salt and pepper to taste

1. Combine ground beef, beaten eggs, and grated potato or breadcrumbs. Shape into balls (size depends on whether being served as main dish or appetizer). Brown in oil, do not crowd. Brown in batches.
2. Combine chili sauce and about half of the jelly. Taste. Add more jelly if needed. Pour sauce mixture over meatballs and let simmer for 30 minutes. Salt and pepper to taste.
3. Serve plain or over rice. Sweet and Sour Meatballs are great as an appetizer. Just make the balls smaller.

Makes about 8 servings

Cook Time: 30 min.

⏳Quick & Easy Meal

✓Instead of browning the meatballs on the stove top, you may bake them in the oven. Place the meatballs on a pan with sides to catch any grease that cooks out. Be sure not to crowd. Bake at 400°F for 15 minutes or until browned. The bake time will vary depending upon the size of the meatballs. Remove to saucepan and continue to Step 2.

BEEF

Bubby's Sweet & Sour Meatballs (M)

Marty Matles

Sauce
1 cup diced celery
2 onions, chopped
1 cup water
1 can (8 oz.) tomato sauce
1 Tablespoon grape jelly
1 teaspoon salt
pepper to taste
1 Tablespoon sugar
2 Tablespoons lemon juice

Meatballs
2 pounds ground beef
3 eggs
1 onion, grated
3 cloves crushed garlic
1 Tablespoon ketchup
2 Tablespoons matzo meal
1/2 teaspoon salt

1. *For sauce*: In a 6-quart pot, mix together all ingredients for the sauce. Heat to boiling, while making meatballs.
2. *For meatballs*: Mix together all meatball ingredients. Wet hands and form balls. Drop them into the boiling sauce. Meatballs should be covered by sauce (if more sauce is needed, prepare additional sauce as in step 1 and add it to the pot). Place lid on pot and cook at least 1 1/2 hours.

Makes 6 to 8 servings

Cook Time: 1 1/2 hours

✍This was a favorite meal at my Bubby's on Chicago's Northside. It is a very "forgiving" recipe...and tastes even better on the second day.

BEEF

Grandma Bonnie's Stuffed Cabbage (M)

Mike & Jake Lacey's Grandma—Bonnie Shacter, Lori Lacey

3 pounds lean ground beef
2 teaspoons salt
3/4 teaspoon pepper
2 teaspoons celery salt
1/2 cup ketchup
2 eggs
1/2 cup crushed unsalted crackers or rice
2 heads green cabbage, about 2 pounds each
3 cups chopped onion
2 bottles (12 oz. each) chili sauce (2 cups)
1 jar (12 oz.) grape jelly
1/4 cup water

1. In a large bowl combine ground beef, salt, pepper, celery salt, ketchup, eggs and crushed crackers (or rice). Mix with hands just until mixture is well combined.
2. Core cabbage, place in large pot and cover with boiling water. Let stand until leaves are flexible, about 5 minutes.
3. Take 1/4 scant cup of beef mix and form into 3x1-inch logs, continuing until all meat is used up (about 28 rolls).
4. Place each meat log on a cabbage leaf and roll.
5. Place chopped onion in greased 12x11x2-inch pan; place rolls on top of onion with seams down.
6. Preheat oven to 375°F.
7. In 2-quart pan, heat and stir chili sauce, jelly and water until smooth. Pour over rolls and cover pan lightly.
8. Bake at 375°F for 2 hours, remove cover and brush with sauce that surrounds the rolls. Bake uncovered for 40 minutes or until sauce is thick and syrupy and the rolls are glazed.

Makes 28 rolls   Oven: 375°F   Bake Time: 2 hr. 40 min.

STUFFED CABBAGE, holishkes in Yiddish, are traditional for Sukkot. Cabbage symbolizes abundance.

BEEF

Helene's Sweet & Sour Stuffed Cabbage (M)

Helene Paris

1 large cabbage
Beef Stuffing
1 pound ground beef
1 1/2 teaspoons salt
1/2 teaspoon pepper
1/2 teaspoon garlic powder
1/4 cup ketchup
3 eggs
1/2 cup uncooked rice
1 medium onion, grated
1/4 cup golden raisins
Sweet & Sour Sauce
1 medium to small onion, chopped
1/2 cup ketchup
1 can (28 oz.) whole peeled tomatoes
1/4 cup sugar (or more to taste)
1/4 cup fresh lemon juice (or less to taste)
1 Tablespoon sweet paprika
1 1/2 teaspoons salt (or more to taste)
6 cups water

1. Freeze cabbage for 2 days. Refrigerate night before to thaw.
2. *For stuffing*: Combine all stuffing ingredients.
3. *For sauce*: In a large pot combine all sauce ingredients, boil and keep simmering until ready to cook cabbage rolls.
4. *To assemble*: Remove core from head of cabbage. Separate leaves. Place one heaping Tablespoon of beef mixture on each leaf. Tuck the ends in and roll up. Place in a 6-quart casserole or a 13x9-inch pan. Carefully pour sauce over cabbage. Cover. Bake at 300°F for 4 hours, then uncover for 1 hour. This is even more delicious the second day.

Make 14 rolls

Freeze Cabbage 2 days. Oven: 300°F   Bake Time: 5 hours

Emmy's Stuffed Cabbage (M)

Emmy Bell

Large head cabbage
Sauce
2 Tablespoons fat or vegetable oil
2 onions, sliced
3 cups canned tomatoes
1 1/2 teaspoon salt
1/2 teaspoon pepper
3 Tablespoons honey or brown sugar
1/4 cup lemon juice
1/4 cup raisins
Stuffing
1 to 1 1/2 pounds ground beef
1/3 cup uncooked rice
1 onion, grated
2 eggs
1/3 cup cold water

1. Soften and separate leaves of cabbage.
2. *For sauce*: Heat fat in deep heavy saucepan. Add onions and brown lightly. Add tomatoes, salt and pepper. Cook, covered, over low heat for 30 minutes.
3. *For stuffing*: Mix together all stuffing ingredients.
4. Place some meat mixture on each cabbage leaf. Tuck in the sides then roll up carefully. Shred remaining cabbage and line bottom of roasting pan with it. Place stuffed cabbage on top of shredded cabbage. Cover with sauce. Cover and cook over low heat or bake at 350°F for 1 1/2 to 2 hours.
5. Add honey or brown sugar, lemon juice and raisins to sauce. Mix in gently. Cover and cook another 30 minutes.

Makes 14 rolls

Oven: 350°F   Bake Time: 2 to 2 1/2 hours

CHICKEN

Roasted Lemon Chicken (M)

Linda Duffié

1 whole (4 pounds) chicken
2 lemons
fresh basil, chopped
oregano, thyme or rosemary; your preference
1 stick (4 oz.) margarine, softened
salt & pepper to taste
small potatoes

1. Wash and pat dry chicken, removing giblets and neck. Keep and freeze giblets and neck for chicken soup or chopped liver.
2. Grate the zest of 1 lemon. Cut in half and squeeze out juice (save halves). In a bowl combine lemon zest and juice, basil, oregano, and margarine to make a paste. Divide into 4 portions.
3. Using one portion of the paste, smear the inside of the cavity, salt and pepper and place lemon halves in cavity.
4. With your fingers, carefully separate the skin from the chicken. Spread two portions of the paste under the skin of the whole chicken.
5. Slice remaining lemon and line roasting pan. Place chicken on top. Surround with potatoes. Smear potatoes with remaining portion of paste.
6. Bake at 450°F for 45 to 60 minutes or until juices run clear from the thickest part of the thigh. Let chicken rest for 10 minutes before slicing.

Makes 4 servings

Oven: 450°F   Bake Time: 45-60 min.

🖩Passover Recipe

Teri-Duck Marinade for Meat or Poultry (P)

Janice Saks

1/2 cup duck sauce
1/4 cup teriyaki sauce
Small amount of honey
Pinch of ginger
6 drops sesame oil
Fresh garlic

1. Mix all ingredients together.
2. Pour over meat or poultry and marinate for 48 hours.
3. Grill or roast as usual.

Makes marinade for about 3 pounds of chicken

Marinate 48 hours

Honey Curry Chicken (M)

Rabbi Myra Soifer

1/4 cup margarine
1/2 cup honey
1/4 cup prepared mustard
1 teaspoon salt
1 teaspoon curry powder
Cut-up chicken

1. Melt margarine in baking pan. Stir in remaining
   ingredients except chicken.
2. Roll chicken parts in mixture. Leave skin side up.
3. Bake at 375°F for 1 hour.

Makes 4 servings

Oven: 375°F   Bake Time: 1 hour

▤Passover Recipe

Chicken with Vegetable Stuffing (M)

Elizabeth Kempler

2 Tablespoons vegetable oil
2 medium onions, diced
2 carrots, diced
2 large stalks celery, diced
1/2 green pepper, diced

1 cup matzo meal
1 egg
Salt to taste
Paprika

1 whole chicken (about 4 pounds)

1. Heat oil and add onions, carrots, celery and green pepper. Stir until lightly browned. Cool.
2. Add matzo meal, egg, salt and paprika. Place stuffing into whole chicken and bake at 350°F about 1 1/2 hours.

Makes 4 servings

Oven: 350°F   Bake Time: 1 1/2 hours

▤Passover Recipe

▤Delicious as a poultry stuffing at Passover — or any time!

Carly, age 12

CHICKEN

Chicken Breasts with Matzo-Farfel Stuffing (M)

Linda Kutten

1 Tablespoon olive oil
1 large onion, diced
1 1/2 cups diced celery
8 ounces white mushrooms, finely chopped
1 1/2 cups crumbled matzo (about 4 sheets)
1 1/2 cups matzo farfel
3 Tablespoons toasted pine nuts (optional)
1/4 cup chopped Italian flat-leaf parsley
1 teaspoon and 2 teaspoons paprika
1/2 teaspoon ground ginger
1/2 teaspoon dried oregano
1/2 teaspoon dried thyme
1/8 teaspoon white pepper
3 egg whites
1 3/4 cups no fat, low salt chicken broth
8 skinless chicken breast halves, rinse & trim fat
Juice of 1 lemon
1 teaspoon garlic powder
1 teaspoon onion powder
white pepper to taste

1. Cook together olive oil, onion, celery, and mushrooms in large skillet until onion is transparent.
2. Toast matzo crumbs and farfel under broiler until golden then add to onion mixture.
3. Mix into onion-matzo mixture pine nuts, chopped parsley, 1 teaspoon paprika, ginger, oregano, thyme, pepper, egg whites and chicken broth. Mix well then spread onion-matzo mixture evenly into oiled 13x9-inch baking dish. Arrange chicken breast halves on top. Sprinkle over chicken breasts lemon juice, garlic powder, onion powder, 2 teaspoons paprika, and pepper. Bake at 350°F for 1 hour.

Makes 8 servings   Oven: 350°F   Bake Time: 1 hour

▤Passover Recipe

CHICKEN

Classic Arroz con Pollo (M)

Adrienne Tropp

2 Tablespoons olive oil
1 chicken, cut-up
2 cups uncooked rice
1 cup chopped onion
1 medium red bell pepper, chopped
1 medium green pepper, chopped
1 clove garlic, minced
3/4 teaspoon and 3/4 teaspoon salt
1 1/2 teaspoons dried basil
4 cups chicken broth
1 Tablespoon lime juice
1/8 teaspoon ground saffron OR 1/2 teaspoon ground
    turmeric
1 bay leaf
2 cups chopped tomatoes
1/2 teaspoon ground black pepper
1 cup fresh or frozen green peas
Fresh basil for garnish

1. Heat oil in large Dutch oven over medium-high heat until
   hot. Add chicken and cook until browned on both sides,
   about 10 minutes. Remove chicken. Keep warm
2. To Dutch oven add rice, onion, red pepper, green pepper,
   garlic, 3/4 teaspoon salt, dried basil. Cook and stir until
   vegetables are tender and rice is browned, about 5 minutes.
3. Add broth, lime juice, saffron and bay leaf. Bring to boil.
4. Stir in tomatoes. Arrange chicken on top and sprinkle with
   3/4 teaspoon salt and pepper. Cover. Reduce heat to low.
   Cook 20 minutes.
5. Stir in peas. Cover and cook until fork can be easily
   inserted into chicken and juices run clear, about 10 minutes.

Makes 8 servings.

Cook Time: 45 min.

CHICKEN

Cranberry Chicken (M)

Marilyn Kurzman

2 bottles (8 fl. oz. each) Russian dressing
1 envelope (1.4 oz.) dried onion soup mix
2 cans (16 oz. each) whole cranberry sauce
12 pieces chicken breasts and thighs

1. Mix together dressing, soup mix and cranberry sauce.
   Spoon and spread some of the sauce mixture on the
   bottom of a 13x9-inch baking pan.
2. Place chicken pieces on top of sauce. Pour remaining sauce
   over the top. Bake, uncovered, at 350°F for 1 1/2 hours.

Makes 6 to 8 servings

Oven: 350°F   Bake Time: 1 1/2 hours

✓I use Wishbone® Russian Dressing.

✓May be prepared ahead for several hours before baking. Keep
refrigerated until ready to bake.

Carly, age 12

Hawaiian Style Chicken (M)

Shirley Rutkovitz

1/4 cup margarine
1 chicken, cut-up into serving pieces
1 can (9 oz.) pineapple slices
2 Tablespoons chili sauce
1 teaspoon soy sauce
1/3 cup ketchup
1/4 cup packed brown sugar
2 Tablespoons cornstarch
1 teaspoon salt
1/4 cup vinegar
1/2 teaspoon Worcestershire sauce

1. Melt margarine in shallow roasting pan. Roll chicken in margarine to coat well. Arrange pieces, skin side up in a single layer in pan.
2. Reserve 2 slices pineapple to garnish. Dice remaining slices and set aside.
3. Mix pineapple juice with remaining ingredients. Cook and stir until thickened, stirring constantly. Add drained pineapple pieces. Spoon half of the sauce over the chicken. Cover and bake at 350°F for 20 minutes.
4. Uncover and bake for 30 to 40 minutes longer or until chicken is tender. Baste chicken as needed with remaining sauce. Garnish with reserved pineapple slices.

Makes 4 to 6 servings

Oven: 350°F   Bake Time: 60-70 min.

CHICKEN

Indian Green Chili Chicken (M)

Deborah Achtenberg

1 ounce tamarind (walnut-size) OR 2 Tablespoons lemon
    juice
hot water
1 1/2 teaspoons sugar
1/4 teaspoon and 3/4 teaspoon salt
vegetable oil
12-15 fresh OR dried curry leaves
2 cups (8 oz.) cups shallots, peeled and finely sliced
6-7 cloves garlic, pressed
1 1/2 inch fresh ginger, peeled & finely chopped
7 hot green chilies (5 cut in thin rings, 2 cut in long slivers)
2 small tomatoes, chopped
1/2 teaspoon ground turmeric
1/4 to 1/2 teaspoon cayenne pepper
3 pounds chicken, skinned , cut-up into small pieces
1 1/4 cups water

1.   Soak tamarind in hot water to cover. Add sugar and 1/4 teaspoon salt.

2.   Heat oil in a heavy pan on Medium-High. When hot, add curry leaves and let sizzle for a couple of seconds. Add shallots, garlic, ginger and the 5 chilies cut into rings. Stir-fry 5 minutes, until shallots are lightly browned. Add tomatoes, cook until soft and browned. Stir in turmeric & cayenne pepper.

4.   Stir in chicken, 3/4 teaspoon salt and water. Simmer 20 minutes, covered tightly, stirring once. Add green chili slivers. Cover, cook for 5 minutes. Mix tamarind mixture and stir in gently. Cook, uncovered, over Medium for 10 minutes to reduce sauce while spooning sauce over chicken. Be sure chicken does not stick to bottom of pan. Spoon fat off before you serve.

Makes 4 servings   Cook Time: 40 min.

▤Passover Recipe

✡In Cochin, India it is served for Shabbat dinner with rice or Indian bread. Use processed tamarind.

Moroccan Chicken with Honey (M)

Adrienne Tropp

> 2 Tablespoons margarine
> 2 Tablespoons vegetable oil
> 8 small chicken breast halves
> salt and pepper
> 2 medium onions, chopped
> 1 clove garlic, chopped
> 1 cup ground almonds
> 1 Tablespoon dried basil
> 1/2 teaspoon pepper
> 1/2 cup honey
> 1 1/2 cups chicken broth
> 2 Tablespoons cornstarch
> Juice of 1 lemon

1. In a casserole dish, heat margarine and oil. Brown chicken on both sides. Season with salt and pepper. Remove chicken.
2. In remaining oil in casserole dish, cook onions and garlic until translucent. Add almonds, basil, pepper and honey. Cook and stir over low heat until well mixed.
3. Combine broth and cornstarch. Add to casserole. Cook and stir over high heat until sauce thickens. Remove from heat stir in lemon juice. Put browned chicken breasts in sauce. Spoon sauce over to coat. Bake covered in preheated 350°F oven for 1 hour or until chicken is tender.

Makes 8 servings

Oven: 350°F   Bake Time: 1 hour

✡Sweet, nice for Rosh Hashanah. Good with bulgur and salad.

✓The casserole may be covered and refrigerated after step 4 and baked later. Just increase baking time.

Chicken with Orange-Pecan Rice (M)

Rabbi Myra Soifer

1 package (6.25 oz.) fast-cooking long grain and wild
    rice
2 cups orange juice
1/4 cup chopped pecans
1 jar (2 oz.) diced pimentos, drained (optional)
4 skinless, boneless chicken breast halves
chopped fresh parsley, if desired

1. Preheat oven to 350°F. Grease an 8-inch square-baking
   pan.
2. Mix rice, seasoning packet included with rice mix, orange
   juice, pecans and pimentos in pan. Place chicken on rice.
3. Cover and bake at 350°F for 35 to 45 minutes or until liquid
   is absorbed and juice of chicken is no longer pink when
   center of thickest piece is cut.
4. Sprinkle with parsley and serve.

Makes 4 servings

Oven: 350°F   Bake Time: 35-45 min.

⌛Quick & Easy Meal

✐All you need is a salad to serve with this dish.

✓ If you have someone in your household allergic to nuts, try
substituting dried cranberries; it's a good combination of
flavors.

Honey-Mustard Chicken with Cashews (M)

Rabbi Myra Soifer

4 skinned, boned chicken breast halves (about 4 oz each)
3 Tablespoons flour
1/2 teaspoon pepper
vegetable cooking spray
1/3 cup reduced-sodium chicken broth
2 Tablespoons honey
2 Tablespoons spicy brown mustard
1/4 cup chopped dry-roasted cashews

1. Cut chicken breast halves into 2x1-inch strips.
2. Combine flour and pepper. Dust chicken strips.
3. Spray a medium nonstick skillet with cooking spray. Heat over medium-high heat. Add chicken, sauté until browned.
4. Reduce heat to medium. Add chicken broth, honey and mustard. Simmer uncovered for 10 minutes.
5. Stir in cashews. Serve over rice, if desired.

Makes 4 servings

Cook Time: about 20 min.

GARLIC

LEMONS

BREAD CRUMBS

CHICKEN

Anna, age 12

Oven-Fried Chicken (M)

Adrienne Tropp

2 large chicken breast halves
1 Tablespoon margarine
1 Tablespoon lemon juice
1/4 teaspoon garlic powder
1/4 cup dry bread crumbs

1. Preheat oven to 375°F.
2. Rinse chicken and pat dry with paper towels. In small frying pan, melt margarine. Add lemon juice and garlic powder.
3. Dip chicken pieces, one at a time into the mixture to coat all over. Then dip into bread crumbs.
4. Place "skin" side up on ungreased baking sheet. Cover with foil. Bake, covered, at 375°F for 30 minutes. Remove foil and continue baking 20 minutes longer or until chicken is nicely browned.

Makes 2 servings

Oven: 375°F   Bake Time: 50 min.

Stefan, age 12

Chicken Adobo (M)

Linda Kutten

3 chicken breast halves, skinned and boneless
2 Tablespoons red wine
3 Tablespoons soy sauce
1/4 cup vinegar
6 cloves garlic, mashed
1/4 teaspoon black pepper
1 bay leaf

1. Place chicken in skillet, be sure skillet is large enough so that the chicken is in one layer.
2. Add all remaining ingredients. Bring to boil. Cover. Reduce heat to medium low (just so chicken simmers slowly). Cook 10 minutes, turn pieces over. Cover. Cook another 10 minutes. Remove all from skillet, saving cooking liquid. Spray skillet with cooking oil. On high heat, brown chicken lightly in pan.
3. Remove chicken to platter. Keep warm.
4. Pour cooking liquid back into skillet. Boil to thicken. Serve over chicken.

Makes 3 servings

Cook Time: 30 minutes

⧖ Quick & Easy Meal

✓ Instead of browning chicken in skillet, brown chicken under broiler or on grill.

✓ If chicken pieces other than boneless breast are used, cooking time will be lengthened.

CHICKEN

Chicken Chutney-Curry Salad (M)

Linda Kutten

2 limes
1 cup mayonnaise
1/4 cup mango chutney
2 teaspoon curry powder
4 cups cubed cooked chicken breast, chilled
2 cups diced celery
1 cup thinly sliced green onions
lettuce leaves
1 can (8 oz.) sliced pineapple, drained
1 can (11 oz.) mandarin oranges, drained

1. Grate zest from one lime. Squeeze juice from 2 limes.
3. Combine lime zest, lime juice, mayonnaise, mango chutney, and curry powder.
4. In a large bowl, place chicken cubes, celery and green onions. Pour mayonnaise mixture over and toss. Serve on a bed of lettuce leaves, top with halved pineapple slices, and mandarin orange sections.

Makes 6 to 8 servings

⌛Quick & Easy Meal

▤Passover Recipe

✓Be sure the chicken breast cubes, pineapple, and mandarin oranges are well chilled.

Hot Chicken Little Salad (M)

Shirley Rutkovitz

2 cups chopped cooked chicken
2 cups chopped celery
1/2 cup chopped toasted almonds
1/2 teaspoon salt
1 Tablespoon minced onion
2 Tablespoons lemon juice
1 cup mayonnaise
1 2/3 cups croutons

1. Combine chicken, celery, almonds, salt, onion, lemon juice and mayonnaise. Toss lightly. Pour into a casserole dish (or make 4 individual casseroles.)
2. Top with croutons.
3. Bake at 450°F for 10 minutes or until hot.

Makes 4 servings

Oven: 450°F   Bake Time: 10 min.

⌛Quick & Easy Meal

✎This recipe was handed down to me by Elaine Sager.

✓Be sure to toast the almonds. It really develops the flavor.

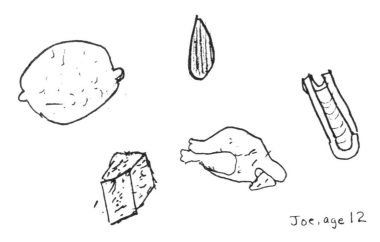

Joe, age 12

Szechwan Chicken (M)

Adrienne Tropp

3 Tablespoons chili sauce
2 Tablespoons sherry
2 tablespoons soy sauce
1/2 cup water
1 teaspoon cornstarch
1/2 teaspoon crushed red pepper
3 skinless, boneless chicken breast halves, cut into 1 1/2-
    inch cubes
1 Tablespoon vegetable oil
1 clove garlic, crushed
1 thin slice of fresh ginger root, finely chopped
9 scallions, sliced into 1 1/2-inch pieces

1. Mix chili sauce, sherry, soy sauce, water, cornstarch and red
   pepper in a small bowl. Add chicken and marinate.
2. In a wok or frying pan, heat oil, garlic and ginger. Drain
   marinated chicken. Add chicken and quickly stir-fry until
   all sides are white. Remove chicken from oil and set aside.
3. Stir-fry scallions about 2 minutes. Return chicken to pan.
   Pour sauce over. Cook and stir until just thickened.
   Remove from heat and serve.

Makes 3 servings

Cook Time: 10 min.

⧗Quick & Easy Meal

Chicken with Curry and Tomatoes (M)

Adrienne Tropp

2 small whole chicken breasts, skin and bone removed
2 teaspoons dry sherry
2 teaspoons cornstarch
2 teaspoons vegetable oil
1 clove garlic, crushed
up to 1/2 teaspoon salt
1 teaspoon curry powder
1 cup snow pea pods
1 firm tomato, cut in large chunks
1 teaspoon powdered chicken bouillon
1/4 cup boiling water

1. Cut chicken breasts into 1/2-inch wide strips. Marinate in sherry and cornstarch for at least 30 minutes.
2. Heat oil and brown garlic. Add marinated chicken and cook quickly, just until chicken turns white. Sprinkle with salt and curry powder, adjusting seasonings to taste.
3. Remove chicken from pan. In the same pan, quickly stir-fry pea pods until heated through, about 1 to 2 minutes.
4. Return chicken to pan. Add tomatoes. Mix chicken bouillon with water and add to chicken mixture. Cook until bubbly.

Makes 3 servings

Marinate: 30 min.   Cook Time: about 10 min.

⧖ Quick & Easy Meal

Braised Spicy Chicken (M)

Linda Kutten

1/4 teaspoon black pepper
3 chicken breast halves, skinned
1 Tablespoon olive oil
1 onion, sliced
1 teaspoon chopped fresh ginger
1/4 teaspoon cinnamon
1/4 teaspoon cardamon
1/8 teaspoon cayenne
1 clove garlic, sliced
1/2 cup dry white wine
3 dates, chopped

1. Sprinkle pepper all over chicken. Brown in oil in hot skillet. Remove chicken.
2. Add onions and brown.
3. Stir in ginger, cinnamon, cardamon, cayenne and garlic.
4. Return chicken to skillet. Pour in wine and add dates. Cover and cook 15 minutes or until chicken is cooked through. If there is too much liquid in the skillet, remove cover and let liquid cook away. Salt to taste.

Makes 3 servings

▤ Passover Recipe

⧗ Quick & Easy Meal

✓ To keep ginger fresh, wash well then freeze in a freezer bag. Whenever you need the ginger, merely shave off what you need. The frozen ginger as a whole is difficult to chop but you will be able to shave off very thin slices that add zest to your cooking. It's much better than using the dried ground ginger.

FISH

Pesto Crusted Salmon (D)

Adrienne Tropp

Pesto
1/3 cup fresh basil leaves
1/3 cup plain, dry bread crumbs
3 Tablespoons pine nuts
3 Tablespoons freshly grated Parmesan cheese
2 garlic cloves
1 Tablespoon olive oil
salt & pepper to taste

About 2 1/4 pounds salmon fillets

1. Preheat oven to 400°F.
2. In food processor combine basil, bread crumbs, pine nuts, Parmesan cheese, and garlic. Process until finely chopped.
3. With the food processor on, in a steady stream add the olive oil until smooth. Season to taste with salt and pepper.
4. Spread pesto mixture evenly on flesh side of salmon.
5. Heat oven-safe skillet on medium high. Place in hot skillet salmon, pesto side down. Cook until pesto is well browned, about 2 minutes.
6. Carefully turn salmon over. Place skillet in 400°F oven for 10 minutes or until just cooked through. Do not overcook.

Makes 3 servings

Oven: 400°F   Bake Time: 10 min.

⧗Quick & Easy Meal

✓If you have pesto on hand, use it. Just add bread crumbs to it.

Salmon with Fruit Salsa (P)

Adrienne Tropp

FISH

2 salmon fillets (about 3/4 pound total)
1/8 teaspoon black pepper
1 Tablespoon olive oil

Fruit Salsa
1/2 cup diced canned pineapple
1 Tablespoon fresh lemon juice
1/2 medium banana, diced
1/2 Tablespoon apricot jam or orange marmalade
2 1/2 Tablespoons minced red onion
1/2 teaspoon hot pepper flakes
1 Tablespoon coconut flakes, optional

1. Remove skin from salmon or have it done for you at the fish counter. Brush oil and grind pepper on each side. Grill, broil, microwave or bake salmon until desired doneness.
2. Meanwhile, combine salsa ingredients.
3. Serve hot cooked salmon with a big dollop of fruit salsa.

Makes 2 servings

⌛Quick & Easy Meal

Cantor Glaser's Poached Salmon (P)

Rabbi Myra Soifer

Salmon fillet (allow 1/2 to 3/4 pound per serving)
Frozen canned orange juice, defrosted

1. Place salmon in pan that fits the salmon snugly.
2. Cover salmon completely with orange juice.
3. Heat over Medium to bring juice to a gentle boil. Lower heat and simmer for approximately 10 minutes.
4. I like the consistency of broiled, rather than poached, salmon; so, I finish this off by placing the salmon under the broiler for 2-3 minutes.

Cook Time: 13 min.

▤Passover Recipe   ⧗Quick & Easy Meal

Puff Pastry Salmon (D)

Rose Orenstein

Parchment paper
1 package (17.3 oz.) frozen puff pastry sheets, thawed
Salmon fillet without skin (about 3 pounds)
1 package (8 oz.) cream cheese, cut in chunks
Fresh dill
Fresh spinach

1. Line cookie sheet with parchment paper. Preheat oven to 450°F.
2. Roll out puff pastry and place on parchment paper. Or you may roll out the puff pastry on the parchment paper on the cookie sheet.
3. Place salmon on one half of the pastry. Top with cream cheese chunks. Sprinkle dill over. Pack a lot of spinach on top. Fold puff pastry over and seal. Cut slits on top. Bake at 450°F for 30 minutes.

Makes about 6 servings   ⧗Quick & Easy Meal
Oven: 450°F   Bake Time: 30 min.

Dilled Salmon & Pasta (P)

Adrienne Tropp

4 small salmon fillets (about 4 oz. each)
1 teaspoon and 1 teaspoon dilly salt-free seasoning
1 package (12 oz.) linguini
1 1/2 cups fresh asparagus, cut into 1-inch lengths
1/4 cup margarine, melted
1/2 teaspoon salt

1. Rinse salmon and pat dry. Sprinkle lightly with dill seasoning.
2. Place on well-oiled grill over medium-hot coals. Grill for 5 to 7 minutes per side or until salmon reaches 145°F in the thickest part and flakes easily with fork.
3. Meanwhile, cook linguini in boiling salted water until tender, about 6 minutes. Drain and set aside.
4. Cook asparagus in boiling water for 3 to 4 minutes or until just tender-crisp. Drain. Add to pasta.
5. Combine melted margarine with 1 teaspoon dilly seasoning and salt. Toss with pasta and asparagus to coat well. Divide into 4 portions on plates. Top each with the grilled salmon.

Makes 4 servings

Cook Time: about 15 min.

⌛Quick & Easy Meal

David, age 12

Heavenly Snapper (D)

Adrienne Tropp

2 red snapper fillets (4 oz. each)
1/4 cup mayonnaise
1/4 cup butter, softened
1/2 cup grated Parmesan cheese
3 Tablespoons chopped green onion
3 dashes Tabasco hot sauce

1. Place fish in a lightly buttered baking dish with skin side down. Bake at 425°F for 12 to 15 minutes per inch of thickness.
2. Mix together mayonnaise, butter, Parmesan cheese, green onion and Tabasco. Spread mayonnaise mixture over top of cooked fish. Broil until top is browned and bubbly.

Makes 2 servings

Oven: 425°F & Broil   Cook Time: about 15 min.

▤Passover Recipe

⧗Quick & Easy Meal

David, age 12

FISH

Sole Amandine (P)

Adrienne Tropp

6 pieces (4 oz. each) sole
flour to coat
1 teaspoon vegetable oil
2 Tablespoons low calorie margarine
1 Tablespoon low calorie margarine
juice of 1 lemon
1 clove garlic, minced
1/4 cup slivered almonds
1/4 cup white wine
1 Tablespoon chopped parsley
pepper to taste

1. Dust sole with flour.
2. Heat oil and 2 Tablespoons margarine in skillet large enough to hold sole. Sauté 2 to 3 minutes on each side to brown. Remove sole and sprinkle with lemon juice.
3. Melt 1 Tablespoon margarine in skillet over medium heat. Add garlic, almonds, and wine. Cook and stir briskly for 30 seconds until light brown. Spoon over sole. Sprinkle with parsley and pepper.

Makes 6 servings

Cook Time: about 7 min.

⏳Quick & Easy Meal

FISH

VEGETABLES

Three-Bean Cholent (P)

Linda Kutten

1/3 cup dried white Northern beans
1/3 cup dried kidney beans
1/3 cup dried lima beans
1/3 cup pearl barley, rinsed
1 Tablespoon dried thyme
1 1/2 teaspoons dried rosemary
1 teaspoon ground coriander
1 teaspoon dried mint leaves
1/2 teaspoon ground pepper
2 cloves garlic, chopped
1 large onion, diced
2 carrots, diced
2 stalks celery, diced
1/2 cup white wine
3 cups water
salt and pepper

1. Rinse Northern beans, kidney beans and lima beans. Cover with 2-inches of cold water and let soak overnight.
2. Place in 4-quart slow cooker pot drained soaked beans and all remaining ingredients in the order given.
3. Cover. Cook on high for 6 to 8 hours. Salt and pepper to taste.

Makes 5 servings

Soak beans overnight   Slow Cook Time: 6-8 hrs.

CHOLENT is a slow cooked meal. It cooked overnight to midday in the oven. This is an updated version, cooked in the slow cooker. The mint, coriander, rosemary and thyme impart a subtle-melded flavor.

Gisela's Red Cabbage   (P)

Richard M. Eisenberg

1 to 2 small heads red cabbage
2 Tablespoons margarine
dash salt and pepper
1 Tablespoon vinegar
2 apples, peeled, cored and quartered
1 Tablespoon sugar
1/2 Tablespoon flour

1. Cut each head of cabbage in half. Remove the thick core. Shred the cabbage. Rinse.
2. In a large saucepan bring to boil enough water to cover the cabbage. Add cabbage. Cook 10 minutes. Drain cabbage.
3. In the now empty pan, heat margarine and a little water. Add cabbage. Cook covered over low heat for 30 to 45 minutes, stirring often. Do not allow cabbage to burn.
4. Add salt and pepper to taste. Add vinegar and apple. Continue cooking until apples are soft.
5. Add sugar. Stir well. Sprinkle flour over mixture and stir to slightly thicken. Adjust to taste by adding more sugar or vinegar.

Makes about 6 servings

Cook Time: 40 to 55 min.

▤Passover Recipe

✍We had this dish for all major holidays. Aunt Gisela Eisenberg Strauss was born in 1911 in Germany near Dresden and is over 90, living in Santa Rosa, CA. Gisela prepares the Red Cabbage without a written recipe, using a little of this and a little of that, so you may take liberties.

VEGETABLES

Cabbage Strudel (D)

Kathryn Karp

>2 Tablespoons butter
>2 Tablespoons vegetable oil
>4 Tablespoons flour
>3 cups chopped onions
>4 medium heads cabbage, shredded
>1/3 cup firmly packed brown sugar
>2 Tablespoons paprika
>salt & pepper to taste
>1 package (16 oz) frozen filo dough
>2 cups (1 pound) butter, melted
>2 cups bread crumbs
>1 egg, beaten (optional)

1. Melt butter and oil in large pot on Low. Add flour, stir and cook until browned. Add onion, cook and stir about 10 minutes, until limp. Add shredded cabbage, brown sugar, paprika, salt and pepper. Cook 45 minutes until tender.
2. Place 4 sheets of filo dough one on top of the other. Fold in half and close like a book. Open first "page," brush with melted butter and sprinkle with crumbs. Turn "pages" and repeat brushing with butter and sprinkling with crumbs until you get to center. Leave center undone. Close "book" and open again from the back. Brush each page with butter and sprinkle with crumbs. When you get to the center, brush with butter and sprinkle with crumbs. Spread 1/4 of the cabbage filling across the bottom of the coated filo dough. Fold ends over and roll jelly roll-fashion. Brush with melted butter.
4. Repeat step 2 to make three more rolls. Refrigerate until butter hardens. May be frozen at this point. Brush with beaten egg, optional. Score at 2-inch intervals through the first layer of dough to allow the steam to escape. Bake at 350°F for 45 minutes. Slice immediately. Serve hot with sour cream and fresh dill. Also, tastes great reheated.

Makes 16-24 servings
Cook Time: 55 min.   Oven: 350°F   Bake Time: 45 min.

VEGETABLES

Sweet Potato Stuffed Cabbage (P)

Janice Saks

1 small cabbage
5 sweet potatoes (baked and mashed)
1 cup pineapple chunks
2 apples, chopped
3/4 cup raisins
1 1/2 teaspoons cinnamon
1/2 cup walnuts, chopped (optional)
1 can (15 oz.) tomato sauce
1 cup water

1. Steam head of cabbage in pot until leaves are soft. Carefully remove whole steamed leaves and set aside.
2. Pre-heat oven to 375°F.
3. Mix together mashed sweet potatoes, pineapple, apples, raisins, cinnamon and walnuts.
4. Put 1/4 cup of mix in center of each leaf and fold ends in.
5. Lay in deep baking pan with folded cabbage ends down.
6. Mix tomato sauce with water and pour over cabbage so leaves remain moist.
7. Bake at 375°F for 30 minutes and serve warm.

Makes 4 to 6 servings

Oven: 375°F   Bake Time: 30 min.

▤Passover Recipe

▤Passover is often a difficult time for me, food-wise, because I'm a vegetarian and all my main staples are not kosher for Passover. A friend gave me some recipes that are kosher for Passover— and vegetarian. This is one of my favorites.

Carrot Ring (P)

Shirley Rutkovitz

2 Tablespoons fine breadcrumbs
1 cup flour
1/2 teaspoon baking soda (optional)
1 teaspoon baking powder
1/2 teaspoon salt
1/2 cup shortening
1/2 cup firmly packed brown sugar
1 egg
2 cups finely grated carrots

1. Grease well 4-cup ring mold. Dust with fine breadcrumbs.
2. Sift together flour, baking soda, baking powder and salt. Set aside.
3. Mix together shortening and brown sugar. Add egg. Mix well.
4. Mix in flour mixture. Fold in carrots. Pour into prepared ring mold. Bake at 350°F for 1 hour.

Makes 4 to 6 servings

Oven: 350°F   Bake Time: 1 hour

VEGETABLES

Carly, age 12

Honeyed Baby Carrots (P)

Julie Stage

1 Tablespoon vegetable oil
1 small onion, chopped
16 ounces baby carrots
2 Tablespoons honey
2 teaspoons grated fresh ginger OR 1/2 teaspoon
    ground ginger
1 Tablespoons minced, fresh parsley

1. Heat oil in a medium saucepan. Add onion and carrots
   and fry over high heat until onions are beginning to brown
   about 3 to 4 minutes. Reduce heat to medium.
2. Stir in honey and ginger. Cover and cook, stirring
   occasionally, until carrots are tender, about 15 minutes.
3. Garnish with parsley and serve hot.

Makes 4 - 6 servings

Cook Time: about 20 min.

Passover Recipe

My daughter Danielle found this recipe in a Jewish cookbook
and made it. We found it to be delicious, but I've never been
able to get her to prepare it again! I have, however, and it's
really special!

stefan, age 12

VEGETABLES

Tsimmes for Rosh Hashanah (P)

Marty Matles

4 sweet potatoes, peeled and chopped into 1-inch
    chunks
3 carrots, peeled and sliced
1 large apple, chopped into 1/2-inch cubes
1 large onion, finely chopped
2 cups prunes, pitted and chopped
1 cup orange juice
1/4 cup honey
Juice of 2 lemons
1 teaspoon salt
1/2 teaspoon cinnamon

1/4 cup fine bread crumbs or matzo meal

1. In a large bowl, combine all ingredients except for the bread
   crumbs. Mix well.
2. Transfer to a large casserole or baking dish. Sprinkle bread
   crumbs on top and then cover with foil or lid. Bake in
   preheated 350°F oven for 1 1/2 to 2 hours, or until
   ingredients are very tender. Uncover for last 20 minutes or
   so, to ensure the top browns well.

Makes 6 servings

▤Passover Recipe

Oven: 350°F   Bake Time: 1 1/2 to 2 hours

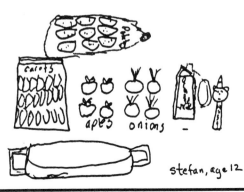

stefan, age 12

Herbed Peas (P)

Carisse Gafni

1/4 cup margarine
4 green onions, sliced
1 package (10 oz.) frozen peas
1 Tablespoon chopped parsley
1/2 teaspoon thyme
1/2 teaspoon sugar
1/4 teaspoon marjoram
1/4 to 1/2 teaspoon salt, to taste

1. Heat margarine in saucepan. Add onions and cook about 5 minutes, until soft.
2. Add frozen peas, parsley, thyme, sugar, marjoram and salt. Stir, cover and heat for about 5 minutes until peas are tender. (For more color, add 1 Tablespoon of chopped pimiento.)

Makes 4 servings   Cook Time: 10 min.
▤Passover Recipe   ⧗Quick & Easy

Spinach Casserole (D)

Marilyn Kurzman

4 packages (10 oz. each) frozen chopped spinach
1 envelope (1.4 oz.) dried onion soup mix
1 pint sour cream
1/3 cup grated Parmesan cheese
1 can (2.8 oz.) French fried onion rings

1. Cook spinach according to package directions. Place cooked spinach in colander and press out all liquid.
2. Combine dried spinach, onion soup, and sour cream. Pour into baking dish (can be refrigerated at this point and finished later).
3. Top with Parmesan cheese and onion rings. Bake, uncovered, at 350°F for 45 minutes.

Makes 8 servings   Oven: 350°F   Bake Time: 45 min.

Mushroom Stuffed Peppers (P)

Linda Platshon

6 green peppers
2 cups sliced mushrooms
1 large onion, chopped
2 Tablespoons margarine or oil
1 cup cooked rice
1/3 cup chopped parsley
1 can (8 oz.) tomato sauce
garlic salt
black pepper
paprika
lemon juice
1 can (8 oz.) tomato sauce

1. Cut off top of peppers and remove seeds. Drop peppers into boiling water to blanch, just till tender-crisp. Do not overcook. Remove peppers, drain and let cool on greased baking pan.
2. Brown mushrooms and onion in margarine. Add rice, parsley, and 1 can tomato sauce. Add garlic salt, pepper, paprika and lemon juice to taste. Mix well.
3. Fill peppers in baking dish with rice mixture. Pour remaining can of tomato sauce over peppers.
4. Bake at 350°F for 1 hour.

Makes 6 servings

Oven: 350°F   Bake Time: 1 hour

✓For a sweet & sour flavor mix 1 Tablespoon brown sugar with 1/2 cup water and pour over peppers.

Yam Casserole (P)

Ruth Dickens & Debbie Pomeranz

4 large yams
1/4 cup granulated sugar
1/2 cup firmly packed brown sugar
1/2 cup water
1/2 cup orange juice
2 Tablespoons margarine
1/4 cup Triple Sec orange flavored liqueur
marshmallows

1. Boil yams till tender, peel and slice.
2. In a saucepan boil sugar, brown sugar, water, orange juice,
   margarine and triple sec, until slightly thickened.
3. Lay slices of yam in a greased 13x9-inch baking dish.
   Slowly pour syrup over. Cover with foil. Bake at 350°F for
   25 minutes.
4. Top with marshmallows and bake another 5 minutes.

Makes about 12 servings

Oven: 350°F   Bake Time: 30 min.

⌛Quick & Easy

✓Can be prepared a day before and refrigerated. Prepare up to
covering with foil, then refrigerate. Bake 45 minutes if very
cold.

Anna, age 12

NOODLES & KUGELS

Mom's Kasha Varnishkas (D or P)

Debbie Baer

1 onion, diced
3 Tablespoons chicken fat, butter, or oil
1 1/2 cup kasha (buckwheat groats)
1 egg slightly beaten
3 cups boiling water
1 package (8 oz.) bowtie noodles
1 teaspoon salt
pepper to taste

1. Brown onion in oil and set aside.
2. In a deep saucepan or large skillet, lightly toast kasha while mixing it with the slightly beaten egg.
3. Add boiling water. Do not cover the pot. Simmer until all water is absorbed.
4. Cook bowties according to package directions.
5. Add browned onions and bowties to the kasha. Add salt and pepper to taste.

Makes 6 to 8 servings

✑I got this recipe from my mother. She got the recipe from her grandmother, so actually we have been making Kasha Varnishkas for over 50 years... and it still tastes good.

📑KASHA is toasted buckwheat groats.

📑VARNISHKA is butterfly in Yiddish. For cooking, it is a bowtie or butterfly shaped pasta.

Kasha Varnishkas by Kathy (D or P)

Kathryn Karp

1 egg
1 cup kasha (buckwheat groats)
2 cups vegetable stock or water
1/2 cup chopped onion
1 cup sliced mushrooms (optional)
2 tablespoons butter or margarine
1/2 teaspoon salt
1/4 teaspoon ground black pepper
8 ounces bow-tie or square egg noodles

1. In small bowl, beat egg. Stir in kasha. Set aside.
2. Heat the stock to simmer. Leave on simmer until ready to use.
3. Meanwhile, in a large, heavy skillet, lightly sauté onions and mushrooms in butter until the onions are lightly browned.
4. Add egg-coated kasha to skillet. On high heat, stir and chop kasha with a fork or wooden spoon for 3 minutes until the egg has dried and the kasha kernels are almost separate.
5. Quickly and carefully add hot stock, leaning away from the skillet to avoid being splattered.
6. Stir in salt and pepper.
7. Cover with a tightly fitting lid. Reduce heat to low and steam kasha for 10 to 15 minutes. Check to see if all the liquid has been absorbed. If not, steam for a few minutes more.
8. Meanwhile, cook the noodles in boiling salted water until tender. Drain and set aside.
9. When the kasha is done, add the drained noodles to the skillet and toss. Add more salt, pepper and butter to taste. Serve piping hot.

Makes 4 to 6 servings   Cook Time: about 30 min.

✓ Serve with beets and fresh applesauce.

NOODLES & KUGELS

Vegetable Lasagna (D)

Selma Goldstein

1 package (8 oz.) lasagna noodles
2 Tablespoons vegetable oil
1 medium onion, chopped
8 ounces mushrooms, sliced
3 zucchini, shredded
4 carrots, shredded
1 teaspoon dried basil
1 teaspoon dried thyme
1 teaspoon dried oregano
1 jar (32 oz.) marinara sauce OR béchamel sauce
2 packages (10 oz. each) frozen chopped spinach, thawed
8 ounces ricotta cheese
12 ounces shredded mozzarella cheese
1/4 cup grated Parmesan cheese

1. Cook noodles in a 6-quart pan with 3 quarts boiling water for 6 to 10 minutes until tender to bite. Adding some oil prevents boil over and keeps noodles from sticking to each other. Drain well.
2. In same pan, cook over high heat stirring often oil, onion, mushrooms, zucchini, carrots, basil, thyme, and oregano until veggies are soft and liquid evaporates, about 5 to 8 minutes.
3. Squeeze liquid out of thawed spinach, mix with ricotta cheese.
4. In a shallow 3-quart baking dish spread a third of marinara sauce. Arrange half of the noodles over sauce. Spread in layers half of onion mixture, half of spinach mix, and half of mozzarella cheese. Repeat layers: sauce, noodles, onion mixture, spinach mixture, mozzarella and ending with sauce. Sprinkle with Parmesan cheese. (At this point you may cover, refrigerate and hold to bake the following day.)
5. Bake uncovered at 400°F for 50 minutes or until hot in the center. Let stand 5 minutes before serving.

Makes 6 servings

Oven: 400°F   Bake Time: 50 min.

NOODLES & KUGELS

Baked Ziti (D)

Linda Kutten

1 package (16 oz.) ziti pasta
1 medium onion, chopped
1 teaspoon olive oil
2 cloves garlic, minced
1 can and 1 can (14 1/2 oz. each) diced tomatoes
1/4 cup red wine
1 tub (15 oz.) low fat ricotta
1 cup and 1/2 cup reduced fat shredded mozarella
    cheese
2 Tablespoons and 2 Tablespoons grated Parmesan
    cheese
1/2 cup skim or soy milk
1/3 cup chopped fresh Italian parsley
1/3 cup chopped fresh basil (or 1 Tablespoon dried)

1. Cook ziti according to package directions.
2. Cook onion and oil in skillet for 5 minutes or until softened. Add garlic and cook 1 minute longer. Add 1 can tomatoes and wine, simmer 10 minutes.
3. In food processor or blender, blend till smooth ricotta, 1 cup mozarella, 2 Tablespoons Parmesan and milk.
4. Drain ziti. Stir in tomato and cheese mixtures. Add parsley, basil and the second can of tomatoes. Toss. Pour into 9x13-inch baking dish.
5. Sprinkle top with remaining 1/2 cup mozarella and 2 Tablespoons Parmesan cheeses. Bake at 400°F for 20 minutes or until lightly browned and hot.

Makes 12 servings   ⌛Quick & Easy Meal

Oven: 400°F   Bake Time: 20 min.

✓If preparing for a small family, split the casserole into three 1 1/2-quart baking dishes and freeze without cheese topping. To serve, thaw in microwave oven, High for 4 minutes, stir. Sprinkle with cheeses, bake at 400°F for 15 to 20 minutes.

NOODLES & KUGELS

Carrot Kugel (P)

Nancy Simkin

    4 eggs, separated
    1/2 cup sugar
    1 cup grated carrots
    1/4 cup grated apple
    1/4 cup red wine
    2 Tablespoons lemon juice
    1/2 teaspoon grated lemon zest
    1/3 cup flour

1. Preheat oven to 375°F.
2. Beat egg whites until stiff and set aside.
3. Beat egg yolks and sugar until light.
4. Combine remaining ingredients and blend into yolk mix.
5. Fold egg whites into carrot mixture and pour into a greased 2-quart casserole dish.
6. Bake at 375°F for 30 minutes or until golden.

Makes 4 – 6 servings

Oven: 375°F   Bake Time: 30 min.

▤Passover Recipe

✡A perfect side dish for Rosh Hashanah (or any festive meal).

▤KUGEL is a pudding usually served as a side dish with the meal. It can be made from noodles, vegetables, or matzo. It can be sweet or savory.

NOODLES & KUGELS

Potato Kugel (P)

Elizabeth Kempler

1 pound boiling potatoes
2 eggs, separated
2 Tablespoons sugar
Juice 1/2 lemon & grated zest
2 Tablespoons chopped almonds
1 teaspoon salt

1. Cook potatoes and grate.
2. Beat egg whites until stiff. Set aside.
3. Beat egg yolks and add to potatoes, along with sugar, lemon juice and zest, almonds and salt.
4. Fold beaten egg whites into potato mixture. Pour into greased 9x9-inch pan.
5. Place pan in a larger pan of boiling water in the center of oven. Bake in preheated 350°F oven for 30 minutes.

Makes about 6 servings

Oven: 350°F   Bake Time: 30 min.

▤Passover Recipe

chloe age 8

Savory Potato Kugel (P)

Linda Kutten

1/4 cup margarine
2 pounds potatoes (about 8 medium or 4 large)
1 large onion
4 eggs
4 Tablespoons matzo meal
3/4 teaspoon salt
1/4 teaspoon pepper

1. Preheat oven to 375°F. Place margarine in shallow 2-quart baking dish. Heat in oven to melt margarine. Tilt dish to grease bottom and sides of pan. Set aside.
2. Peel and shred potatoes and onion. (Use the food processor to make the job easier.)
3. Beat eggs in food processor till foamy. Add matzo meal, salt and pepper.
4. Return a portion of the shredded potato/onion mixture to food processor bowl. Process, just to mix and breakup some of the large shreds. Mix in remaining potato/onion mixture.
5. Pour on top of melted margarine in baking dish. Bake at 375°F for 50 to 60 minutes, until golden brown.

Makes 8 servings

Oven: 375°F   Bake Time: 50-60 min.

▤Passover Recipe

✓To make mini-muffin kugels which are great as appetizers, melt the margarine and brush liberally onto mini-muffin tins. Spoon mixture into buttered tins, filling level with top. Bake at 375°F for 40 to 50 minutes. Remove immediately from pan. Serve hot. (May be frozen. To reheat, place frozen cooked nuggets on cookie sheet and bake at 375°F for 20 minutes.) Makes about 48 minis.

NOODLES & KUGELS

Grandma Sada's Noodle Kugel (D)

Marty Matles

8 ounces cream cheese
4 eggs
1 1/2 cups milk
8 ounces sour cream
1/2 cup butter
1 teaspoon vanilla
1/2 cup sugar
1 Tablespoon cinnamon
1 cup golden raisins or dried cranberries
1 package (12 oz.) wide egg noodles, cooked and
      drained
1 cup crushed frosted flakes cereal
Additional cinnamon to sprinkle over top of Kugel

1. Blend together cream cheese, eggs, milk, sour cream, butter, vanilla, sugar and cinnamon. Add cranberries or raisins.
2. Mix together with the cooked noodles.
3. Pour into 13x11-inch greased baking pan. Sprinkle with crushed frosted flakes and cinnamon.
4. Bake in 325°F oven for 1 hour 15 minutes. Cool and cut into squares. Serve warm.

Makes 15 servings

Oven: 325°F   Bake Time: 1 hr. 15 min.

✓ Steve's grandmother shared this kugel with me. I've added golden raisins to it or dried cranberries.

✓You can safely substitute non-fat items for the milk, sour cream and cream cheese.

✓Egg substitute or egg whites work fine too. But the butter needs to be there!

NOODLES & KUGELS

Shirley's Noodle Kugel (D)

Shirley Rutkovitz

1 package (12 oz.) egg noodles
1/4 pound butter or margarine, softened
1/2 cup sugar
1 cup cottage cheese
2 cups sour cream
1/2 teaspoon salt (if desired)
2 teaspoons vanilla
5 eggs
cinnamon

1. Preheat oven to 350°F. Grease a 13x9-inch baking dish and set aside.
2. In a large saucepan, cook noodles, drain and set aside.
3. In a large bowl, beat together butter and sugar until smooth. Add cottage cheese, sour cream, salt and vanilla. Mix in eggs, one at time, beating well after each addition.
4. Stir in cooked noodles and pour into greased baking dish.
5. Sprinkle top with cinnamon. Bake at 350°F for 50 to 55 minutes or until golden brown. Let stand 15 minutes before cutting into squares.

Makes about 15 servings

Oven: 350°F   Bake Time: 50 to 55 min.

✓ May be served hot or cold and can be frozen. Serve with extra sour cream if desired.

NOODLES & KUGELS

Grandma Honey's Pineapple Noodle Kugel (D)

Lori Lacey

1/2 pound medium-wide noodles, cooked
2 eggs
1 can (15 oz.) crushed pineapple, drained
1 cup sour cream
1/4 pound (one stick) margarine
sugar
crushed corn flakes or frosted flakes

1. Combine noodles, eggs, pineapple and sour cream.
2. Melt butter and pour over noodles.
3. Place in 9x9-inch baking dish and cover with sugar and crushed corn flakes.
4. Bake at 350°F for approximately 1 hour.

Makes about 12 servings

Oven: 350°F   Bake Time: 1 hour

Ben, age 8

Apple Noodle Kugel (D)

Kiersten Mayer

1 package (12 oz.) egg noodles
1/2 cup sugar
1/2 cup raisins
1/2 teaspoon ground cinnamon
2 teaspoons almond extract
1 apple, chopped
2 cups milk
3 eggs
2 Tablespoons and 2 Tablespoons butter or margarine,
　　melted

1. Cook noodles, rinse under cold water and drain well.
2. Place noodles in bowl. Add sugar, raisins, cinnamon,
    almond extract and apples. Mix well.
3. Beat milk and eggs together. Mix in 2 Tablespoons melted
    butter. Pour into noodle mixture. Mix well.
4. Pour into 11x7-inch baking dish. Drizzle remaining
    2 tablespoons butter over top. Bake at 350°F for about
    1 hour until golden brown.

Makes about 12 servings

Oven: 375°F   Bake Time: about 1 hour

✓Kids like it when you add corn flakes or fruit to the top.

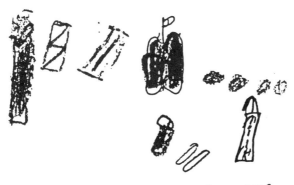

Aaron, age 9

NOODLES & KUGELS

To-Die-for-Kugel (D)

Lynne Daus, Jewish Fest Recipe

8 ounces medium-width egg noodles
1 pound cream cheese
1/2 pound (1 cup) butter
1 pint (2 cups) sour cream, divided
1 teaspoon vanilla
1 cup sugar
8 eggs
1 can (11 oz.) mandarin oranges, drained
1 can (8 oz.) crushed pineapple, drained

Topping
1/3 cup firmly packed brown sugar
4 ounces chopped pecans
1 teaspoon cinnamon
2 Tablespoons butter

1. Cook noodles in boiling water. Drain. Set aside.
2. In food processor, blend cream cheese, butter and 1 cup sour cream until smooth. There must not be any lumps. Mix in vanilla. Pour into mixer bowl.
4. Add and mix well, sugar, eggs, and remaining sour cream.
5. By hand stir in cooked noodles. Fold in mandarin oranges and pineapple. Pour into 13x9-inch baking pan. Bake at 350°F for 50 minutes.
6. *For Topping:* Combine brown sugar, pecans and cinnamon. Sprinkle over top of Kugel. Dot with 2 Tablespoons butter. Bake another 20 minutes until golden. Serve hot or at room temperature.

Makes 18 servings

Oven: 350°F   Bake Time: 70 minutes

✓The kugel may be made ahead, refrigerated, then baked the next day.
✓For a lighter golden brown top, use granulated sugar.

NOODLES & KUGELS

Lower Fat Kugel (D)

Linda Platshon.

1 package (12 oz.) yolkless noodles
1/4 pound butter or margarine, softened
1/4 cup sugar
1/2 pint (1 cup) nonfat cottage cheese
1 pint (2 cups) nonfat sour cream
1/2 teaspoon salt
2-3 Tablespoons vanilla extract
2 whole eggs
3 egg whites
Topping
cinnamon
1/4 cup packed brown sugar
3/4 cups corn flakes, crushed

1. Preheat oven to 350°F. Grease or spray with cooking spray bottom of 13x9-inch baking pan.
2. Cook noodles in boiling water until tender. Drain and set aside.
3. In a large bowl, beat together butter and sugar.
4. Add cottage cheese, sour cream, salt, and vanilla.
5. Mix in eggs and egg whites. Stir in noodles. Pour into baking dish.
6. Combine cinnamon, brown sugar and corn flakes. Sprinkle over top.
7. Bake at 350°F for 50 to 55 minutes or until golden brown. Let stand 5 minutes before cutting into squares.

Makes: 8-12 servings

Oven: 350°F   Bake Time: 50-55 min.

✍A real crowd pleaser.

✓ You can use low-fat cottage cheese and sour cream instead of nonfat.

NOODLES & KUGELS

Savory Egg Noodle Kugel (D)

Julie Stage

1 pound extra wide egg noodles
1 carton (16 oz.) cottage cheese
1 carton (8 oz.) sour cream
5 eggs
1 teaspoon onion powder
2 Tablespoons chopped parsley
4 Tablespoons butter

1. Cook noodles per instructions on bag. Blanch with cold water.
2. Mix together cottage cheese, sour cream, eggs, onion powder and parsley. Toss in cooked noodles.
3. Place butter in 13x9-inch baking pan. Heat in 350°F oven for a few minutes, just to melt the butter completely and heat the pan. By heating the pan with the butter, a crispy bottom is achieved.
4. Pour noodle mixture into hot melted butter pan. Bake at 350°F for 60 minutes.

Makes 15 servings

Oven: 350°F   Bake Time: 60 min.

✍Recipe from my mother, Louise Halprin Wilson. My father never related to the sweet kugel my mother's mother made, and liked this variety best. The rest of the family likes sweet kugel with cinnamon and apples.

✓For a lighter version, use low-fat sour cream and cottage cheese. I've not tried fat-free varieties.

Easy Apple Matzo Kugel (P)

Nancy Daum

4 cups matzo farfel
1 can (21 oz.) apple pie filling
4 eggs, beaten
1 cup raisins
1 teaspoon salt
1 teaspoon cinnamon
nutmeg
margarine

1. Run water over farfel in colander quickly. Don't let it get soggy.
2. Mix all ingredients, except margarine.
3. Spray vegetable cooking spray on an 8x8x2-inch baking dish.
4. Spread mixture in pan. Dot with margarine. Bake at 350°F for 45 minutes or until brown.

Makes about 9 servings

Oven: 350°F   Bake Time: 45 min.

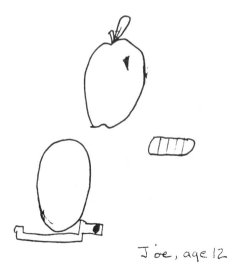

Joe, age 12

Fresh Apple Matzo Kugel (D or P)

Shirley Rutkovitz

4 matzos
water
3 eggs, well beaten
1/2 teaspoon salt
1/2 cup sugar
1/4 cup melted butter or margarine
1 teaspoon cinnamon
1/2 cup chopped walnuts
2 large apples, cored and chopped
1/2 cup raisins
butter to taste

1. Break matzos. Soak in water until soft. Drain.
2. Beat eggs with salt, sugar, butter and cinnamon. Add softened matzos, walnuts, apples and raisins.
3. Pour into baking dish. Dot with butter. Bake at 350°F for 45 minutes.

Makes about 6 servings

Oven: 350°F   Bake Time: 45 min.

▤Passover Recipe

✍This is from my brother, Earl Lutzker

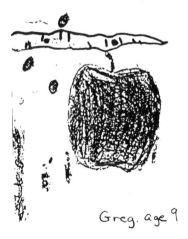

Greg. age 9

Quick Matzo Apple Sugar Substitute Kugel (P)

Nancy Daum

4 cups matzo farfel
1 can (16 oz.) plain apple slices
4 eggs beaten
1 teaspoon salt
1 teaspoon brown sugar sweetener
1 teaspoon cinnamon
1 teaspoon nutmeg
margarine

1. Run water over farfel in colander quickly. Don't let it get soggy.
2. Combine all ingredients, except margarine.
3. Spray vegetable cooking spray on an 8x8x2-inch baking dish. Pour in apple mixture. Dot with margarine.
4. Bake at 350°F for 45 minutes or until brown.

Makes about 6 servings

Oven: 350°F   Bake Time: 45 min.

▤Passover Recipe

✓I use Brown Sugar Twin®. Use more sweetener, if you like it sweeter

NOODLES & KUGELS

Banana Nut Matzo Kugel (D or P)

Elizabeth Kempler

3 cups matzo farfel
4 eggs
1/2 teaspoon salt
6 Tablespoons sugar
1/4 cup melted butter or vegetable shortening
2 medium bananas, sliced
1/2 cup chopped walnuts

1. Pour cold water over farfel and drain immediately so farfel is moist but not soggy.
2. Beat eggs with salt, sugar and melted fat. Mix in farfel.
3. In a greased 1 1/2-quart baking dish, place half of the farfel mixture. Arrange sliced bananas on top and sprinkle with walnuts. Top with remaining farfel mixture.
4. Bake at 350°F for 45 minutes or until set and lightly browned.

Makes 6 servings

Oven: 350°F   Bake Time: 45 min.

Chloe age 8

LATKES AND BLINTZES

- *PANCAKES* -

Easy Blender Potato Latkes (P)

Julie Stage

2 eggs
1/2 small onion
1 teaspoon salt
2 Tablespoons flour
1/4 teaspoon baking powder
4 cups raw cubed potatoes (leave peeling on and cut
    into small cubes)
cooking oil

1. Put eggs, onion, salt, flour, baking powder and 1/2 cup
   potatoes in blender. Pulse on "grate."
2. Add remaining potatoes, 1/2 cup at a time. Do not over
   blend.
3. Fry in hot well greased griddle, making 3-inch circles.
   Delicious with applesauce and sour cream!

Makes: 12 pancakes

Jack, age 8

LATKES are pancakes usually made from potatoes but other
vegetables or matzo can be used. The commonality is that it is
fried in oil. Latkes are traditional food for Hanukkah.

Ronnie's Potato Latkes (P)

Ronnie Varney

onions, 1 small or 1/2 large onion per person
potatoes, approximately 3 per person
eggs, 1 plus per person
matzo meal or flour
salt
pepper

1. Grate onions very fine.
2. Grate potatoes. Experiment with the size of the grate. Some people like the fine grate (mushy), others like them grated like fast food hotcakes.
3. Mix onion, potatoes, eggs, matzo meal, salt and pepper to taste.
4. Spoon mixture onto oil in heated frying pan or griddle. Some cook them with lots of oil, others use non-stick cooking utensils with less oil.
5. Fry until golden brown on both sides (or crispy).
6. Serve with sour cream and apple sauce. Some people even like ketchup and maple syrup.

▤Passover Recipe

✍This recipe has been developed over years of latke parties.

✓Grate onions early and keep in refrigerator.

✓Experiment with the amount of eggs, matzo meal (or flour) until you find the consistency you like.

Blender Potato Latkes (P)

Emmy Bell

Proportions are for one person; multiply as needed:
2 small potatoes, washed and cut up
1/2 large onion OR 1 small onion, peeled and cut up
1 egg
matzo meal
salt and pepper to taste

1. Blend together potatoes, onion and egg until smooth.
2. Add matzo meal to consistency desired.
3. Salt and pepper to taste.
4. Drop by tablespoons onto hot oil. Cook thoroughly on one side, turn over and brown second side. Drain on paper towels. Enjoy!

Passover Recipe

Spinach Popeye Pancakes (P)

Linda Platshon

1 large can (27 oz.) spinach, chopped
2 eggs
1 cup matzo meal
salt
pepper
garlic powder or flakes
light frying oil

1. Combine drained spinach, eggs and matzo meal.
2. Season to taste with salt, pepper and garlic powder. Mix well.
3. Heat oil in skillet. Place about a tablespoon of mixture into hot oil in skillet. Fry well on both sides until golden brown. Drain on towel. Can be served hot or cold.

Passover Recipe   ✓Great as a side dish.

LATKES & BLINTZES

Passover Matzo Pancakes (D)

Tinia Merkin

1 egg white
1 whole egg
1/2 cup water
pinch salt
1 1/2 ounces (about 1/3 cup) matzo meal
2 to 3 tablespoons oil

Topping:
8 ounces fresh spinach, chopped, cooked & drained
2 ounces (1/2 cup) Cheddar cheese, grated
salt and pepper to taste

1. Whisk egg white and egg until thick.
2. Gradually add water and salt.
3. Sprinkle in matzo meal. Beat until smooth.
4. Heat oil in frying pan. Spoon foamy batter onto hot pan, using about 1/4-cup batter per pancake. Be sure to stir batter and scoop from the bottom as the matzo meal tends to settle and the foam rises to the top. Almost immediately, turn and press down slightly. Cook about 1 minute. Place cooked pancakes on baking sheet. Repeat until mixture is used up.
5. In the meantime, combine topping ingredients. Heat broiler.
6. Cover each cooked pancake with spinach topping.
7. Broil 1 minute, until cheese is melted. Serve immediately.

Makes about 8, 4-inch pancakes

Cook Time: few minutes

▤Passover Recipe

✍Spinach and cheese crown light pancakes. Delicious!

✓Instead of topping with spinach mixture, sprinkle with cinnamon and sugar.

Apple Pancake (D)

Adrienne Tropp

1 stick (4 oz.) butter
5 apples, peeled, cored, thinly sliced
1 Tablespoon packed brown sugar

Pancake mixture
6 eggs
1 1/4 cups milk
1 cup flour
3 Tablespoons sugar
1/2 teaspoon salt
1/2 teaspoon cinnamon
1 teaspoon vanilla

1. Melt butter in 9x13-inch baking pan. Spread sliced apples over. Sprinkle with brown sugar. Bake in 425°F oven for about 30 minutes until brown.
2. Beat together eggs, milk, flour, sugar, salt and cinnamon. Mix in vanilla. Pour over hot browned apples. Bake at 425°f for 20 minutes. Serve immediately. The mixture really puffs up and is best eaten right from the oven.

Makes 8 to 10 servings

Oven: 425°F   Bake Time: 50 min.

✓Use any variety baking apple.

LATKES & BLINTZES

Blintz Soufflé (D)

Lori Lacey

1/2 cup butter or margarine
12 frozen blintzes
2 cups sour cream
pinch salt
6 eggs, beaten
2 Tablespoons vanilla
3 Tablespoons sugar
4 Tablespoons orange juice

1. Melt butter in a 13x9-inch glass baking pan.
2. Roll each frozen blintz in butter and place in pan.
3. Combine remaining ingredients and pour over blintzes. Let stand 2 hours before baking.
4. Bake at 350°F for 45 to 60 minutes.

Makes 12 servings

Sit Time: 2 hours before baking

Oven: 350°F   Bake Time: 45-60 min.

BLINTZES are thin pancakes (like crepes) usually stuffed with a cheese filling but other fillings can be used. The filling is totally enclosed—two sides folded in to cover the filling then the blintz is rolled from the non-folded side.

LATKES & BLINTZES

Mom's Cheese Blintzes (D)

Julie Stage

Crepes
3 eggs
1 cup milk
dash salt
1 cup flour
butter for cooking

Filling
1 pound pressed cottage cheese or ricotta cheese
1 package (3 oz.) cream cheese
1 egg
salt

1. *For crepes*: Beat eggs. Add milk, salt and flour. Stir until smooth. Let stand in refrigerator for several hours or overnight.
2. *To cook crepes*: Heat a heavy 8-inch non-stick skillet until water splatters. Swirl small pat of butter until melted. Pour in small amount of batter. Swirl until evenly spread. Cook over medium heat until underside is golden. Carefully turn and cook other side. Turn onto waxed paper to keep warm.
3. *For filling*: Mix filling ingredients.
4. Put a few spoonfuls of filling in center of crepe. Turn in top and bottom edges, roll up. Put seam side down. Serve topped with blueberry or cherry pie filling and sour cream.

Makes: 12-14 blintzes

Crepe Batter Stand Time: several hours to overnight

✓Low fat cottage cheese may be used. I have not tried fat free cream cheese.

✓For sweet blintzes: add to filling 1/3 cup sugar and 1/2 cup yellow raisins.

Emmy's Cheese Blintzes (D)

Emmy Bell

Crepes batter
6 eggs
2 cups milk
1 teaspoon salt
1/4 cup vegetable oil
1 1/2 cups flour
butter

Filling
4 cups pot cheese or dry curd cottage cheese, drained
2 egg yolks
1 1/2 teaspoons salt
2 Tablespoons melted butter
up to 4 Tablespoons sugar, optional

1. For Crepes: In blender, mix eggs, milk, salt and oil. Stir in flour. Heat fry pan with butter over Medium. Use 2-Tablespoons batter for 6-inch pan, 3-Tablespoons batter for 8-inch pan. Tilt pan to coat bottom. Let brown then carefully turn out onto paper towels, browned side up.
2. For Filling: Beat together cheese, egg yolks, salt and butter. Add sugar if you like it sweet. Put a spoonful of filling along one side of the pancake. Fold that side over the cheese. Fold in sides. Roll up.
3. Fry, flap side down first, in a little butter or oil. OR freeze and fry later. Delicious served with sour cream or apple sauce.

Makes 15-20 blintzes

Preparation time: 1 1/2 hours

✓Since I hate leftover egg yolks or whites, I use 2 whites from the filling for the batter in place of one whole egg.

✓I line the kitchen counter with paper towels before I start frying so I can keep turning out the pancakes.

LATKES & BLINTZES

"Lite" Bites (D)

Andi Kaylor

Crepes batter
3/4 cup flour
1 egg
1 egg white
1 cup water
1/4 teaspoon salt

Filling
8 ounces nonfat cottage cheese
8 ounces low fat ricotta cheese
1/4 teaspoon salt
1/2 teaspoon grated orange zest
1/4 teaspoon ground cinnamon
1/8 teaspoon vanilla
2 packets sweetener

1. For Crepes: Beat together crepe batter ingredients until smooth. Let stand 15 to 20 minutes.
2. For Filling: Mix all filling ingredients together and set aside.
3. Heat a 6-inch nonstick fry pan. Spray with butter flavored cooking spray. Pour a scant 1/4 cup of batter into pan and tip so batter spreads evenly over pan. Heat until sides start to pull away. Flip over for a few seconds. Put on plate and fill.
4. Pat a couple of spoonfuls of filling on lower center of crepe. Fold up bottom and then sides then bring over top to form a rectangle.
5. Sauté in butter flavored cooking spray on skillet. Serve with nonfat sour cream and preserves.

Makes about 10 blintzes

Batter Stand Time: 15-20 min.

✓I use Equal® sweetener.

Latkes & Blintzes

Oatmeal-Buttermilk Pancakes (D)

Linda Kutten

2 cups rolled oats, quick or old-fashioned
1/2 cup flour
10 Tablespoons dried buttermilk
3 Tablespoons sugar
1 teaspoon baking powder
1 teaspoon baking soda
1/4 teaspoon salt
2 eggs
1/4 cup butter, melted
2 1/2 cups water
1 teaspoon vanilla
butter for frying

1. In a large bowl stir together dry ingredients: oats, flour, buttermilk, sugar, baking powder, baking soda and salt.
2. Beat eggs. Stir in melted butter, water and vanilla. Pour into dry ingredients. Mix well. Cover and refrigerate about 2 hours or overnight to thicken batter.
3. Heat skillet over Medium. Brush skillet with butter. For each pancake pour 1/4-cup of batter into skillet. Cook until bottoms are golden brown and bubbles form on top. Flip pancakes over to brown. To keep pancakes warm, place on baking sheet in 250°F oven in a single layer. Serve with fresh strawberries or blueberries and syrup or preserves.

Makes about 16 pancakes

Refrigerate batter 2 hours to overnight.

✓Freeze pancakes with waxed paper between to prevent sticking together. To reheat, thaw in microwave oven then heat in toaster for a crisp crust.

✓I always keep dried buttermilk on hand but you may use fresh buttermilk--just substitute 2 1/2 cups buttermilk for the dried buttermilk and water.

LATKES & BLINTZES

QUICK BREADS

Blueberry Muffins (D)

Linda Platshon

1/2 cup lite margarine
3/4 cup sugar
2 eggs
2 cups flour
2 teaspoons baking powder
1/2 cup milk
1 teaspoon vanilla
1 3/4 cups blueberries

1. Cream margarine and sugar. Beat in one egg at a time.
2. Mix together flour and baking powder. Stir into egg mixture, alternately with milk and vanilla.
3. Add blueberries.
4. Pile high in muffin tin lined with paper liners. Bake at 350°F for 30 to 40 minutes.

Makes 12 muffins

Oven: 350°F   Bake Time: 30-40 min.

✓If you have no concerns for lowering fat, you can use butter or regular margarine.

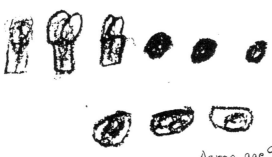

Aaron, age 9

Cranberry Scones (D)

Linda Kutten

1 1/2 cups flour
1 cup rolled oats, quick or old-fashioned
1/4 cup sugar
1 1/2 teaspoons baking powder
1 teaspoon ground ginger
1/2 teaspoon baking soda
1 teaspoon grated lemon zest
1/4 cup unsalted butter
1 1/4 cups dried cranberries
1 cup fat free plain yogurt
1 egg

1. In a large bowl mix together flour, oats, sugar, baking powder, ginger, baking soda, and lemon zest. Cut in butter until mixture resembles coarse crumbs.
2. Stir in cranberries.
3. Combine yogurt and egg. Stir into flour mixture just until dry ingredients are moistened.
4. Divide into two portions. Pat each into 4-inch circles on cooking oil sprayed cookie sheets. Cut each into 4 wedges. Gently spread wedges apart about 1/4-inch.
5. Bake in 400°F oven for 12 to 15 minutes or until golden brown. Serve hot.

Makes 8 scones

Oven: 400°F   Bake Time: 12-15 min.

Passover Granola (P)

Adrienne Tropp

> 2 1/2 cups matzo farfel
> 1 cup shredded fresh coconut
> 1 cup coarsely chopped blanched almonds
> 1/4 cup (1/2 stick) margarine
> 1/4 cup firmly packed brown sugar
> 1/4 cup honey
> 1/2 teaspoon salt
> 1/2 cup raisins (optional)

1. Combine farfel, coconut and almonds in medium bowl. Spread mixture onto greased cookie sheet. Bake in preheated 325°F oven for 15 to 20 minutes until lightly toasted, tossing several times for even browning.
2. Simmer for a few minutes in a 2-quart saucepan the margarine, sugar, honey and salt, stirring constantly. Remove from heat. Mix in well toasted farfel-coconut mixture, tossing the ingredient like a tossed salad, to coat evenly.
4. Spread onto cookie sheet. Bake at 350°F for 20-25 minutes until ingredients are golden brown. Stir frequently to prevent burning. Do not overcook.
5. Pour the hot granola into a large mixing bowl. Stir in the raisins with a flexible spatula to break up any large lumps. Store in airtight container when cooled.

Makes: 4 1/2 cups

Oven: 325°F & 350°F   Bake Time: 15 & 25 min.

▤Passover Recipe

✓May be served with milk for breakfast. Great as a snack or a crunchy topping for cottage cheese, etc.
✓For variations try: chopped dried apples, apricots, peaches or dates in place of raisins; cashew and walnuts in place of almonds; add 1 to 2 teaspoons cinnamon; add 2 to 4 Tablespoons carob flavor; OR add 1 to 2 teaspoons grated orange zest.

QUICK BREADS

Sour Cream Coffee Cake (D)

Nancy Simkin, Jewish Fest Recipe

1 cup butter
1 1/2 cups sugar
3 eggs
1/2 teaspoon vanilla
1 pound sour cream
3 cups flour
1 1/2 teaspoons baking powder
1 1/2 teaspoons baking soda

Nut layer
2 cups coarsely chopped walnuts
3/4 cup sugar
1 1/2 teaspoons cinnamon

1. Beat together butter and sugar until creamy. Beat in eggs and vanilla. Stir in sour cream.
2. Combine flour, baking powder and baking soda. Add to egg mixture. Mix well.
3. Combine nut layer ingredients of walnuts, sugar and cinnamon.
4. Spread half of the batter into 10-inch ungreased tube pan. Layer a half of nut mixture followed by the remaining batter.
5. Bake at 350°F for 60 to 75 minutes or until toothpick inserted in center of dough comes out clean. Cool on rack for 10 minutes before removing from pan.
6. Gently lift from pan to cooling rack, keeping upright. The topping is loose and will scatter. Place on rack with topping side up. Cool completely.

Makes 12 servings

Oven: 350°F   Bake Time: 60 –75 min.

Jewish Coffee Cake (D)

Nadine Lipson

Nut Mixture
1/2 cup firmly packed brown sugar
1 cup ground walnuts
1 teaspoon cinnamon

Batter
4 cups all purpose flour
1/2 teaspoon salt
1 1/2 teaspoons baking powder
1 teaspoon baking soda
1/2 pound (1 cup) butter
1 teaspoon vanilla
2 cups sugar
1 pint (2 cups) sour cream
6 eggs, beaten

1 jar (10 oz.) maraschino cherries, well drained

1. Mix together brown sugar, walnuts and cinnamon.
2. Sift together flour, salt, baking powder and baking soda.
3. Cream together thoroughly butter, vanilla and sugar. Add sour cream. Beat until well blended.
4. Add flour mixture to the creamed mixture alternating with the eggs. Begin and end with flour. Beat well, scraping the bowl frequently.
5. Generously grease and flour a 10-inch tube pan.
6. Pour a third of the batter into the pan, top with a third of the cherries and a third of the nut mixture. Repeat this a second and third time.
7. Bake in preheated 350°F oven for 1 hour 15 minutes or until tests done.

Makes 1 tube cake

Oven: 350°F   Bake Time: 1 hr. 15 min.

Pumpkin Bread (D or P)

Linda Platshon

1 cup sugar
1/3 cup butter or margarine
2 whole eggs
1 cup canned pumpkin
1/3 cup, less 1 Tablespoon cold water
1 2/3 cups flour
1 1/4 teaspoons pumpkin pie spice
1/4 teaspoon baking powder
1 teaspoon baking soda
3/4 teaspoon salt
1/2 cup raisins
2/3 cup walnuts

1/2 tsp alspice
2 tsp cinn
1/2 tsp nutmeg

1. Cream sugar and butter. Add eggs, pumpkin, and water.
2. Sift together flour, pumpkin pie spice, baking powder, baking soda and salt. Mix into pumpkin mixture.
3. Stir in raisins and walnuts.
4. Pour into well-greased and lined 9x5-inch loaf pan. (Disposable aluminum pans work well.) Bake at 325°F for 1 hour.

Makes 6 to 8 servings

Oven: 325°F   Bake Time: 1 hour

✓Coffee may be substituted for cold water.

✓If you desire to cut cholesterol, instead of 2 whole eggs use 1 whole egg and 1 egg white OR 2 egg whites

✓ May be baked in well-greased and floured coffee cans.

✓ Cover with a dish towel for 5 minutes after removing bread from oven. This keeps bread moist.

Date Nut Bread (P)

Ethel Jaffe

3/4 cup finely chopped walnuts
1 cup cut-up pitted dates
1 1/2 teaspoons baking soda
1/2 teaspoon salt
3 Tablespoons shortening
3/4 cup boiling water
2 eggs
1 teaspoon vanilla
1 cup granulated sugar
1 1/2 cups flour

1. Mix nuts, dates, baking soda and salt with fork. Add shortening and water and let stand for 20 minutes.
2. Preheat oven to 350°F.
3. Beat eggs with fork. Beat in vanilla, then sugar. Mix in flour. Stir in date mixture.
4. Pour blended mixture into a greased 9x5-inch loaf pan. Bake at 350°F for 65 minutes or until done.

Makes 1 loaf

Oven: 350°F   Bake Time: 65 min.

QUICK BREADS

Slone's Pump. Bread

1 c. nut
2 1/3 c. sug.
4 eggs
2 scnt cup p. mp
5/3 c water
3 1/3 cup flour

1/2 tsp. bak pwd
1 tsp 11 soda
1 1/2 tsp salt
1 tsp nutmeg
1 tsp vanilla
1 cup nuts
1 tsp cinn.
1/4 clove

Flo's Banana Nut Bread (D)

Barbara Pratt

    3/4 cup sugar
    1 egg
    1/2 cup milk
    3/4 cup chopped walnuts
    1 cup mashed bananas (2 to 3 bananas)
    3 cups all-purpose baking mix

1. Preheat oven to 350°F. Grease 9x5-inch loaf pan.
2. Beat together sugar, egg, milk, walnuts and bananas.
3. Add all-purpose baking mix and beat hard 30 seconds or until mixed well.
4. Pour into greased loaf pan. Bake at 350°F for 1 hour.

Makes 1 loaf

Oven: 350°F   Bake Time: 1 hour

✍My mother-in-law gave this recipe to me. I have used it many times, because it's so easy to prepare and always comes out well!

✓For an all purpose baking mix I like Bisquick®.

✓If desired, add 1/2 teaspoon cinnamon and 1/2 teaspoon vanilla.

YEAST BREADS

Bread Machine Challah (P)

Julie Stage

1/3 cup warm water
2 teaspoons dry yeast or (1 envelope)
1/4 cup frozen concentrated orange juice, thawed
2 large eggs
3 cups flour
3 Tablespoons margarine
1/2 teaspoon salt
4 Tablespoons sugar

egg yolk
poppy seeds or sesame seeds

1. Put bread machine on dough setting.
2. Place all ingredients up to and including sugar in bread machine. Start cycle.
3. When dough cycle is finished, take dough out and divide into 3 equal strands. Braid. Place on a greased cookie sheet. Cover and let rise until double.
4. Brush tops with egg yolk diluted with a small amount of water.
5. Sprinkle with sesame or poppy seeds.
6. Bake at 350°F for 45-50 minutes.

Makes 1 challah

Oven: 350°F   Bake Time: 45-50 min.

✓For a less sweet challah, reduce sugar to 2 Tablespoons.

Hal's Challah (P)

Nancy Daum

1 package dry yeast (rapid is ok)
1 cup warm water (105°F –110°F))
2 to 3 Tablespoons sugar
1 1/2 teaspoons salt
1 egg (room temperature)
yellow food coloring, if desired
2 Tablespoons oil
3 to 3 1/2 cups unbleached flour
raisins
1 egg yolk
poppy or sesame seeds

1. Dissolve yeast in warm water in a large bowl. Add sugar & salt stir well.
2. Beat egg & add. (Add some yellow food coloring, if desired.) Add oil. Beat slightly. Gradually stir in flour, mixing well.
3. Turn out on floured board. Knead for 3-4 minutes, adding flour, if needed, to keep dough from being sticky. Raisins can also be added. Let rise until triple in size.
4. Turn out on floured board. Beat air out. Divide in 4 parts. Let rest 15 minutes.
5. Take 3 of the sections and form into lengths that are then braided and placed on ungreased baking pan. Divide 4th section into 3 smaller sections that are then braided into a smaller piece and placed on top of larger braid. Let rise.
6. Beat egg yolk slightly and brush over loaf. Sprinkle with sesame or poppy seeds. Bake at 350°F for 25 minutes, until nicely browned and sounds hollow when tapped on bottom & sides. Remove and cool on a cooling rack.

Makes 1 challah

Oven: 350°F   Bake Time: 25 min.

✍Hal's been known to add chocolate chips for the kids (and me)!

Jewish Braided Challah (D or P)

Julie Stage

2 packages dry yeast
1 3/4 cups warm water
1 Tablespoon salt
1/2 cup sugar
1/4 cup butter or margarine, melted
3 cups and 4 cups flour
4 large eggs, beaten
sesame seeds or poppy seeds

1. Dissolve the yeast in water. When it bubbles (about 5 minutes) add the salt, sugar and butter. Blend in 3 cups flour and eggs. Beat thoroughly.
2. Add the remaining flour, mixing in with your hands. Turn onto floured board and knead until smooth and elastic. Place in greased bowl. Cover and let rise until doubled.
3. Punch the dough down and turn onto floured breadboard. Divide dough in half. Cut one half into 3 equal pieces. Roll into strips about 18 inches long. Braid the strips and place on greased cookie sheet.
4. With the remaining half dough, cut two-thirds of it into 3 equal pieces, roll into strips and braid. Place on top of first braid.
5. Form the remaining dough into a braid or just twist the strip. Lay on top of the second braid.
6. Brush the top of the loaf with melted butter. Do not brush the braids separately or the upper braids will slide off during baking. Cover and let rise until doubled.
7. Brush again with melted butter. Sprinkle heavily with poppy seeds or sesame seeds. Bake at 350°F for approximately 1 hour.

Makes 1 large or 2 small

Oven: 350°F   Bake Time: 1 hour

YEAST BREADS

Laura's Luscious Challah (P)

Laura Ashkin

2 cups lukewarm water
3 packages active dry yeast
8 to 10 cups flour
1 cup and 1/2 cup sugar
1 1/2 teaspoons salt
2 sticks (1/2 pound) margarine
5 eggs, beaten, reserve one for glaze
poppy or sesame seeds

1. Mix water and yeast in a very large bowl. Add 3 cups flour and 1 cup sugar. Stir with fork and let rise 30 minutes in a warm place.
2. Put 5 cups flour, salt, and 1/2 cup sugar in food processor bowl. Pulse a few times. Cut margarine into small pieces. Add to flour in food processor bowl. Process until mixture is the consistency of cornmeal. Set aside.
3. To yeast mixture, add 4 beaten eggs. Stir well. (Mix will decrease in volume.) Add flour-margarine mixture to yeast mixture and work in bowl. Gradually add up to 2 cups more flour, adding a little at a time. Once you can handle the dough, knead it on a floured board. Keep adding a little flour at a time as you knead until it is no longer sticky. Knead for 10 minutes, adding flour as needed. (Depending on the weather and your flour, you may use 1 to 2 cups extra flour.)
4. Put the dough in an oiled bowl and cover with a towel. Let rise in a warm place for 2 hours or until doubled and a hole poked with your finger does not bounce back.
5. Punch down. Knead lightly for a minute or two. Divide dough into 4 equal parts to make 4 loaves. (A kitchen scale helps.).
6. Braid the loaves. A four-part braid is a bit tricky, but weighing to be sure each part is equal helps.
7. Cover and let rise as long as possible, 3 to 5 hours is fine.

8. Brush top with reserved beaten egg. Sprinkle with poppy or sesame seeds. Bake at 350°F for 30 minutes.

Makes 4 challahs

Oven: 350°F   Bake Time: 30 minutes

✓Do not let the bread rise in too warm a place, as they can collapse. Also, be gentle with the risen breads—don't joggle them too much.

✓Be sure the egg for the glaze is at room temperature.

✓ A kitchen scale helps in dividing the dough into equal parts.

✓You can also make 2 loaves, instead of 4, and make them into circles for Rosh Hashanah. But you will need to increase the cooking time to about 45 minutes.

✓Put two loaves on each pan for baking. After 15 minutes exchange shelves and reverse pans in oven. This will ensure the breads rise evenly.

A rielle, age 12

Jewish Fest Challah (D)

Jewish Fest

1 cup water
2 Tablespoons butter
2 eggs
3 1/2 cups flour
1/2 teaspoon salt
5 Tablespoons sugar
3 teaspoons dry yeast

egg yolk wash (egg yolk & 1 Tablespoon water)
poppy or sesame seeds

1. In the order listed, put all ingredients up to and including yeast in bread machine. Process for dough only, through first rise.
2. Take dough from bread machine. Divide dough into 4 portions. Divide each portion into 3 more portions. Form into long rolls. Braid 3 rolls onto cookie sheet lined with parchment paper. Let rise in warm place.
3. Brush tops with egg yolk wash. Sprinkle with poppy or sesame seeds. Bake at 350°F for 20 minutes or until browned.

Makes 4 mini challahs

Oven: 350°F   Bake Time: 20 minutes

✓For one large loaf, divide dough into 3 portions then braid.

Healthy Whole Wheat Challah (D or P)

Sharon Honig-Bear

2 Tablespoons dry active yeast
1/2 cup and 1 1/2 cups warm water
pinch of sugar
1/2 cup oil or melted butter or margarine
1/2 cup honey
3 eggs
1/2 teaspoon salt
3 to 4 cups all purpose flour
3 cups whole wheat flour

egg yolk
sesame or poppy seeds

1. In a small bowl, dissolve yeast in 1/2 cup warm water with a pinch of sugar. Let it stand until yeast bubbles.
2. In a large bowl, mix oil, honey, eggs and 1 1/2 cups water. Add yeast mixture. Add salt and 2 cups each of all purpose flour and whole wheat flour. Stir.
3. Add remaining cup of whole wheat flour and 2 -3 cups all-purpose flour. Knead until smooth. Add additional flour as necessary. Let rise in greased bowl, covered, for about 1 hour.
4. Cut into 4 portions. Shape each into a loaf. Glaze tops with egg yolk. Sprinkle with seeds. Let rise.
5. Bake at 350°F until brown and crusted, about 30 minutes.

Makes: 4 challahs

Oven: 350°F   Bake Time: about 30 min.

✍ A "Great Harvest" type loaf using whole-wheat flour.

Bread Machine Rye Bread (D)

Andi Kaylor

1 3/4 cups water
3 1/2 cups bread flour
1/2 cup rye flour
2 Tablespoons nonfat dry milk
2 Tablespoons sugar
2 teaspoons salt
2 Tablespoons butter
2 teaspoons yeast
2 teaspoons gluten
1 1/2 teaspoons caraway seeds
1 1/2 teaspoons fennel seeds.

1. Place all ingredients in bread machine.
2. Follow manufacturer's instructions to start cycle to make and bake bread.
3. Enjoy!

Makes 1 loaf

YEAST BREADS

Leah, age 9

Sufganiyot (Filled donuts for Hanukkah) (D)

Sharon Honig-Bear

2 1/2 cups flour
1 package fast-rising yeast
1/4 cup sugar
1/3 teaspoon salt
1/3 teaspoon cinnamon
3/4 cup lukewarm milk
2 egg yolks
2 Tablespoons butter
Vegetable oil for frying
Powdered sugar
Apricot preserves, jam, filling or icing.

1. Place flour, yeast, sugar, salt and cinnamon in food processor. Process briefly to mix. Add milk, egg yolks and butter. Process until dough forms a ball. Process 45 seconds more (may be mixed by hand if butter is soft).
2. Place dough on lightly floured board and knead about a minute. Put in greased bowl, cover and let rise in warm place until doubled, about 1 1/4 hours.
3. Punch down on floured board, cover loosely and rest for 5 minutes. Roll out thinly (about 1/4 inch) and cut into 2-inch rounds. Place on a cookie sheet, cover with a towel and let rise in warm place for 15 minutes.
4. Heat 2-inches of oil to 375°F and drop in rounds near edge of pan without crowding. Turn when underside is golden brown, about 3 minutes. Fry until the other side is brown, then remove and drain on paper towels.
5. When cool enough to handle, make a small slit in the side of each pastry, using a small spoon, insert a filling like preserves, Nutella® or icing. Roll in powdered sugar.

Makes: about 2 dozen   Oil: 375°F   Fry Time: about 5 min.

✡Make sufganiyot, an Israeli alternative to latkes. Participants can assembly line-style make the sufganiyot.

YEAST BREADS

Pizza (D)

Linda Kutten

1/2 teaspoon salt
3 Tablespoons vegetable oil
3 Tablespoons nonfat dry milk solids
3 cups flour, 1 cup at a time
1 pagage dry yeast
1 cup hot water (115°F)
Topping
shredded mozarella cheese
4 mushrooms, sliced
1/2 green pepper, thinly sliced
1/2 onion, thinly sliced
bottled pasta sauce or pizza sauce

1. Combine in mixing bowl, salt, oil, nonfat dry milk, 1 cup flour and yeast.
2. Stir in hot water. Add remaining flour, 1 cup at time. Mixing well.
3. Knead on floured board until not sticky. Form into a ball and place in greased bowl. Cover and let rise in a warm place for 20 minutes.
4. Divide dough in half. Pat each half onto a 12-inch round greased pizza pan.
5. Sprinkle mozzarella cheese over dough. Top with mushrooms, pepper and onion. Drop spoonfuls of sauce over all.
6. Bake at 425°F for 20 minutes.

Makes 2, 12-inch pizzas

Oven: 425°F   Bake Time: 20 min.

✓The toppings are just suggestions. Put the vegetables you like. Just be sure to slice them thin.

✓Placing the cheese before all the rest of the ingredients keeps the crust crisper.

COOKIES

Hamantaschen (shortbread-type) (P)

Linda Platshon

2 cups sifted flour
6 Tablespoons sugar
1 1/2 teaspoons baking powder
Pinch of salt
2 eggs, beaten
3 Tablespoons vegetable oil

prepared fillings: prune, poppy, fruit, etc.

1. Sift together dry ingredients. Make a depression in center, add eggs and oil. Mix thoroughly.
2. Roll out to 1/8" thickness on a lightly floured board. Cut into rounds about 3" in diameter. Place about 1 teaspoon. of filling in the center of pastry round. Bring sides together high in center to make triangle and pinch to seal in filling.
3. Bake on a greased baking pan at 350°F until golden brown, about 10 minutes.

Makes 1 dozen

Oven: 350°F   Bake Time: 10 minutes

PURIM & HAMANTASCHEN. The springtime holiday of Purim celebrates the rescue of the Jews from genocide at the hands of the evil Haman, as told in the Book of Esther. One of the most popular Purim delicacies is hamantaschen, a cookie traditionally filled with poppy seeds or prune filling. Some have suggested that the three-cornered shape of the hamantaschen is meant to recall the distinctively-shaped hat of Haman. Less traditional, but more kid-friendly, are fruit flavors, using preserves or fruit pie fillings.

Rabbi's Purim Hamantaschen (D)

Rabbi Myra Soifer

1/2 cup butter
1 cup sugar
1 egg
1 Tablespoon milk
1 teaspoon vanilla
2 cups flour
2 teaspoons baking powder
1/4 teaspoon salt

fruit filling of your choice

1. Cream butter. Add sugar. Beat until fluffy.
2. Add egg, milk, and vanilla. Beat well.
3. Sift together flour, baking powder, and salt. Add to butter-sugar-egg mixture. Blend thoroughly. Chill for 20 minutes.
4. Roll on floured board until 1/8-inch thick. Cut into circles (Rabbi's tip: I use a drinking glass that is slightly larger than 2-inches in diameter, and it seems to make hamantaschen just the right size!)
5. Fill with fruit filling of your choice. (Another tip: Less filling works much better than too much. P.S. We kids don't much like poppy seed and prune. Strawberry, blueberry, and apple are favorites. Chocolate would be great, but I haven't figured out how to make that work yet)
6. Crimp three corners to make a triangular shape. Place on greased cookie sheets. Bake at 400°F for 10 minutes.

Makes: 3 dozen

Oven: 400°F   Bake Time: 10 min.

Fest Hamantaschen (P)

Linda Platshon, Jewish Fest Recipe

1 1/3 cups vegetable shortening
1 cup sugar
2 eggs
6 Tablespoons water
1/2 teaspoon vanilla
4 cups flour

poppy seed or prune filling (recipes follows)

1. Cream together shortening and sugar.
2. Beat eggs, one at a time. Beat until smooth.
3. Stir in water and vanilla.
4. Mix in flour until dough forms a ball. Form into 4 balls and refrigerate overnight.
5. Roll out on floured board to 1/8 inch thick. Cut into 3 inch circles. Fill with 1 teaspoon filling. Pinch together 3 corners to make a triangular shape.
6. Bake on parchment lined cookie sheet at 375°F for 15 minutes or until golden brown.

Makes: 2 dozen

Oven: 375°F   Bake Time: 15 min.

Arielle, age 12

Mohn (Poppy seed) Filling (P)

Jewish Fest

8 ounces poppy seed
1/2 cup honey
2 Tablespoons sugar
1 egg
1 orange, zest and juice

1. Place all ingredients in saucepan.
2. Boil for a few minutes. Cool. May be frozen.

Makes 1 1/2 cups (enough for 2 batches of hamantaschens)

Prune Filling (P)

Jewish Fest

4 ounces pitted prunes
1/4 cup raisins
1 teaspoon lemon juice
1/4 teaspoon lemon zest
2 Tablespoons sugar
1 teaspoon honey

1. Soak prunes overnight in cold water or 2 hours in hot water.
2. Drain. Place in food processor and remaining ingredients. Blend till smooth.

Makes 3/4 cup (enough for 1 batch of hamantaschens)

Chocolate Hamantaschen (D)

Jewish Fest recipe

6 Tablespoons butter
1 cup sugar
1 egg
2 squares (1 oz. each) unsweetened chocolate, melted
1 teaspoon vanilla
1 1/2 cups flour
1/2 teaspoon baking soda
1/4 teaspoon salt
chocolate chips
hot fudge sauce

1. Cream together butter and sugar until smooth. Add egg and continue beating until light and fluffy. Stir in melted chocolate and vanilla.
2. Combine flour, baking soda and salt. Mix into chocolate mixture until all blended.
3. Form into 4 balls. Roll each ball between plastic wrap. Do not use flour, as it will whiten the dough. Cut into 3-inch circles. Place in center of each circle, a teaspoon of hot fudge sauce and 3-4 chocolate chips. Bring 3 edges up to form a triangle. Press edges together, leaving a small opening to view filling. Place 1-inch apart on parchment lined cookie sheet.
4. Bake at 350°F for10 to 12 minutes. Cool on cooling rack while on parchment. Cookie is very soft and will break easily until it is cool.

Makes about 20

Oven: 350°F   Bake Time: 10-12 min.

✓Do not refrigerate dough, as it will be impossible to handle. It will fall apart. Also, rolling the dough thicker rather than thinner will be easier to fill and handle.

Fest Mandelbrot (P)

Jewish Fest Recipe

3 eggs
1/2 cup vegetable oil
1 cup sugar
3 cups flour
1/4 teaspoon salt
3 teaspoons baking powder
1 teaspoon vanilla
1 teaspoon almond extract
1/2 cup slivered almonds

Cinnamon-sugar mixture
1/2 cup sugar
2 teaspoons cinnamon

1. Beat eggs well. Add oil and sugar. Beat well
2. Combine flour, salt and baking powder. Mix into egg mixture.
3. Add vanilla, almond extract and almonds. Mix to blend.
4. Shape with well greased hands into three 9-inch rolls. Place on parchment lined jelly roll pan. Sprinkle rolls with cinnamon-sugar mixture. Bake at 325°F for 20 to 25 minutes.
5. Remove from oven and slice on a diagonal into 1/2 inch slices. Slices should be about 5-inches long.
6. Place slices cut side down on parchment lined cookie sheet. Sprinkle tops with cinnamon-sugar. Return to oven and bake at 250°F for 60 minutes, until lightly browned. Turning once. Cool thoroughly before storing.

Makes 25 slices

Oven: 325°F & 250°F   Bake Time: 1 hr 25 min.

📖MANDELBROT means "almond bread" in Yiddish. Many know it as biscotti.

Mandelbrot (P)

Ronnie Y. Varney

3 eggs
1 cup sugar
1 cup oil
1/2 teaspoon almond extract
1/2 teaspoon vanilla
3 cups flour
1/4 teaspoon baking soda

add-ins to taste: small chocolate chips, nuts, raisins
(most like lots of chips and walnuts; some like
almonds, pecans and peanuts)
cinnamon-sugar mixture

1. Mix eggs, sugar, oil, almond extract and vanilla. Then add
   flour and baking soda. Mixture will be thick and sticky.
   Add chips, nuts, or raisins as you desire and mix well.
2. Shape (like a flat football) into three loaves on greased
   cookie sheet (keep hands wet when shaping). Sprinkle with
   a cinnamon-sugar mixture.
3. Bake at 350°F for 30 minutes.
4. Then while still slightly warm slice. Cut down length of
   loaf and then across into slices. Place slices cut-side down
   on cookie sheet. Bake for an additional 10-15 minutes.

Makes: 3 loaves, about 30 slices

Oven: 350°F   Bake Time: 45 min

✓Bake on center rack. If bottoms become too brown, reduce cooking
time or shut off oven on the second bake. Dough can also be shaped
round for large cookies.

✓For a variation: add 2 mashed bananas to mixture before adding
flour.

Glacéd Fruit Mandelbrot (P)

Ruth Dickens

2 eggs, well beaten
1 cup sugar
1/4 cup oil
1/4 teaspoon lemon extract (or almond extract)
1/2 teaspoon vanilla
1/2 cup sifted flour
1/2 cup chopped almonds
1/2 cup chopped glacéd fruit mix
1 1/2 cups sifted flour
1/2 teaspoon salt
1 1/2 teaspoons baking powder

1. Add eggs to sugar. Mix well.
2. Stir in oil, lemon extract and vanilla extract.
3. Sift 1/2 cup flour over chopped almonds and glacéd fruit. Stir into egg-sugar mixture. Mix well.
4. Combine 1 1/2 cups flour, salt, baking powder. Stir into above mixture. Makes a soft, moist dough.
5. Onto a lightly greased cookie sheet, shape with floured hands into two long loaves, about 2-inches wide and 3/4-inches high.
6. Bake at 325°F for 25 to 30 minutes.
7. When slightly cool, cut into 3/4-inch slices. Place slices on their sides on cookie sheet. Return to oven that has been turned off. Leave in oven for 10 minutes to harden slightly. Cool on racks.

Makes 16 slices

Oven: 325°F   Bake Time: 25-30 min.

COOKIES

Passover Chocolate Chip Mandelbrot (D or P)

Emmy Bell

2 cups sugar
1/2 pound butter or margarine
6 eggs
2 3/4 cups matzo cake meal
1/2 teaspoon salt
3/4 cup potato starch
1 bag (6 or 12 oz.) semi-sweet chocolate chips
1 to 1 1/2 cups nuts (walnuts), chopped
1 teaspoon cinnamon
2 teaspoons sugar

1. Cream together sugar and butter.
2. Beat in eggs, one at a time.
3. Combine cake meal, salt and potato starch. Blend into egg mixture.
4. Add chocolate chips and nuts. Mix well.
5. With wet hands, form into 4 loaves, approximately 2-inches wide and 10-inches long. Place on greased cookie sheets.
6. Mix together cinnamon and 2 teaspoons sugar. Sprinkle on loaves.
7. Bake at 350°F for 45 minutes.
8. Slice while warm into 1/2-inch pieces. Wrap in aluminum foil.

Makes: 3 dozen slices

Oven: 350°F   Bake Time: 45 min.

▤Passover Recipe

✓Works best if butter and eggs are at room temperature.

✓Freezes and/or stores well. Tastes delicious!

Rugelach (D)

Wendy Alderman, Jewish Fest Recipe

2 sticks butter, soft
1 package (8 oz.) cream cheese, soft
2 cups flour

apricot preserves or raspberry & mini chocolate chips
cinnamon-sugar mixture
ground walnuts or raisins

1. Blend butter, cream cheese and flour by using fork until they form a dough. Divide dough into four balls, wrap in plastic wrap or waxed paper and refrigerate several hours or overnight.
2. Roll each ball into a round on floured board or cloth. Dough should be thin.
3. Spread with light layer of preserves, sprinkle with cinnamon-sugar, and nuts.
4. Cut into 12 wedges and roll each wedge to the center point, starting at wide end.
5. Place point side down on greased cookie sheet and bake at 375°F for 25 minutes.

Makes 4 dozen

Oven: 375°F   Bake Time: 25 minutes

✓The dough in this traditional pastry is wonderfully tender and lends itself to many improvisations.

✓For Larger Batches: Roll out each ball in a rectangle about 18x4 inches. Spread filling and roll up in a long tube (jelly roll style) and then cut into 1 1/2-inch pieces. Makes 12.

✓You can use a mixer or food processor. First mix together butter and cream cheese then add flour to prevent over-mixing.

COOKIES

Chocolate Caramel-Covered Matzo (D)

Adrienne Tropp

2 to 4 whole Matzo
1 stick butter (1/2 cup)
1/2 cup firmly packed brown sugar
1 bag (6 oz.) chocolate chips

1. Preheat oven to 450°F
2. Place foil on cookie sheets.
3. Place one layer of matzo on foil-lined cookie sheet. Set aside. (Depending on how thick you like the chocolate and caramel layer determines the amount of matzo you use.)
4. In small saucepan, melt butter and sugar. Boil until syrup mixture coats a spoon.
5. Pour hot mixture evenly over matzo. The mixture will spread while baking.
6. Bake at 450°F for 4 minutes.
7. Take cookie sheet out of oven. Sprinkle chocolate chips over matzo. Return to oven for 1 minute.
8. Take cookie sheet out. Spread chocolate to evenly cover matzo. Cool on foil until chocolate hardens then break into pieces. The cooling process can be hastened by refrigerating or freezing. You can use a knife to cut into neat 1 1/2 x 3-inch rectangles but the broken pieces are interesting.

Oven: 450°F   Bake Time: 5 min.

▤Passover Recipe

✓Be sure to place the matzos on aluminum foil as the caramel layer oozes and makes a mess. The foil makes it easier to handle and clean up.

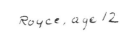

Royce, age 12

Matzo Almond Rocha (D)

Esther Isaac

4 whole matzos
1 cup firmly packed brown sugar
1 cup butter
1 large bag (12 oz.) chocolate chips
sliced almonds, chopped

1. Preheat oven to 350°F. Line cookie sheet with foil, dull side up and grease well. Place whole matzos on foil.
2. Combine butter and sugar in saucepan. Boil for 5 minutes, stirring occasionally. Pour mixture neatly over matzos and spread to cover.
3. Sprinkle each matzo with chocolate chips and bake at 350°F for 5 minutes.
4. Spread the softened chips evenly with a knife. Sprinkle with chopped almonds.
5. Freeze for 1 hour, then break into small pieces. Can store in refrigerator for several days.

Oven: 350°F   Bake Time: 5 min.

Freeze Time: 1 hr.

▤Passover Recipe

▤ A friend brought this dish for Passover one year and it's been a favorite ever since. We make it any time. After all, what do you do with all that left over matzo?

✓Try different flavored chips as there are lots of varieties— peanut butter, caramel, white chocolate, etc. Also instead of almonds try other nuts, sprinkles, M&M's, etc.

Honey Raisin Matzo Cookies (P)

Elizabeth Kempler

1/2 cup vegetable shortening
2 eggs
3/4 cup sugar
1/2 cup honey
1/2 pound raisins
1 teaspoon cinnamon
1 cup matzo meal
1 cup matzo farfel

1. Preheat oven to 350°F.
2. Cream shortening with the eggs, sugar and honey until smooth, light and fluffy.
3. Add raisins and cinnamon, meal and farfel, mixing well.
4. Drop by heaping teaspoons onto greased cookie sheet about 2-inches apart. Cookies will spread.
5. Bake at 350°F for about 20 minutes until browned.

Makes about 40, 3-inch cookies

Oven: 350°F   Bake Time: 20 min.

▤Passover Recipe

✡These are special occasion cookies and pareve (no dairy).

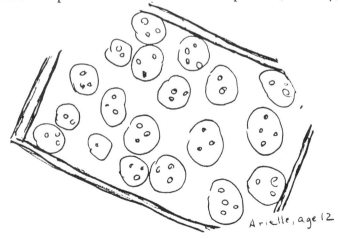

Arielle, age 12

COOKIES

Orange Farfel Cookies (P)

Julie Stage

2 cups matzo meal
2 cups matzo farfel
1 1/2 cups sugar
1 teaspoon cinnamon
pinch salt
3 eggs, beaten
2/3 cup margarine, softened
1 orange, grated zest
1 cup chopped walnuts

1. Mix together matzo meal, matzo farfel, sugar, cinnamon, and salt.
2. Add beaten eggs, margarine, and orange zest. Stir.
3. Add nuts. Mix well. Dough will be slightly crumbly.
4. Shape into rounded teaspoon-sized balls of dough. Place 2-inches apart on greased or oil-sprayed cookie sheet.
5. Bake at 350°F for 10 to 15 minutes.
6. Store cooled cookies in airtight container.

Makes 6 dozen cookies

Oven: 350°F   Bake Time: 10-15 min.

▤Passover Recipe

✍My maternal grandmother, Dora Bolker, made these every year for Passover. My family looks forward to these and it's a nice reminder of Grandma.

▤FARFEL is from the Yiddish farfallen which means fallen away. Matzo farfel is small matzo chips, like confetti. Farfel is also made from noodle dough that is grated, hence fallen away from the grater. The farfel is shaped and sized like barley grains.

COOKIES

Luscious Chocolate-Dipped Macaroons (D)

Barbara Pratt. Jewish Fest Recipe

5 3/4 cups (16 oz.) Angel Flake® coconut
1 can (14 oz.) sweetened condensed milk
2 egg whites
2 teaspoons vanilla
1 package (8 oz.) semi-sweet chocolate squares

1. Preheat oven to 350°F. Line cookie sheets with parchment paper or grease with vegetable shortening or spray vegetable oil.
2. Mix coconut, sweetened condensed milk, egg whites, and vanilla in large bowl until well blended.
3. Drop by teaspoonsful, 1-inch apart, on greased cookie sheet.
4. Bake at 350°F for 15-25 minutes, until golden brown on top but not burnt on bottom.
5. Remove immediately to cooling racks. Cool.
6. Melt semi-sweet chocolate squares, half the package at a time, according to package directions. (Do not melt the whole package at once. It cools too quickly and makes dipping difficult.)
7. When macaroons are cooled, dip halfway into melted chocolate. Place on waxed paper. Chill in refrigerator for one hour to set chocolate.

Makes 3-4 dozen

Oven: 350°F   Bake Time: 15-25 min.

▤Passover Recipe

✍This recipe has been adapted from many recipes I looked through for the First Annual Jewish Fest, 1997.

✓I prefer to keep the cookies in the refrigerator until serving so that the chocolate won't melt.

Aunt Nita Passover Chocolate Chip Cookies (P)

Tinia Merkin

1/2 cup shortening or margarine
1 cup sugar
2 eggs
3/4 cup potato starch
3/4 cup matzo cake meal
1/2 cup orange juice
4 tablespoons matzo meal
1 bag (6 oz.) semi-sweet chocolate chips
3/4 cup chopped nuts

1. Cream together shortening and sugar.
2. Beat in eggs, one at a time.
3. Combine potato starch and cake meal. Add alternately with orange juice. Mix well.
4. Stir in matzo meal, chocolate chips and nuts.
5. Drop by teaspoonsful on greased cookie sheet.
6. Bake at 350°F for 15 minutes or until light brown.

Makes about 4 dozen

Oven: 350°F   Bake Time: 15 min.

▤Passover Recipe

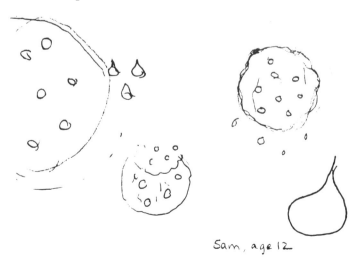

Sam, age 12

Passover Chocolate Chip Cookies (P)

Originally by Adelaide Suplin.

1/2 cup margarine, softened
1 rounded cup sugar
3 eggs
1 cup matzo cake meal
1/4 teaspoon salt
1/2 cup potato starch
1 bag (12 oz.) chocolate chips
3/4 cups toasted walnuts or pecans

1. Preheat oven to 350°F.
2. Beat together margarine, sugar, and eggs.
3. Combine matzo cake meal, salt and starch. Add to egg mixture.
4. Mix in chocolate chips and nuts.
5. Drop by spoonfuls onto greased cookie sheet. Bake at 350°F for 10 to 15 minutes until light golden brown.
6. Immediately remove from pan and cool. Store in airtight container. These cookies freeze well.

Makes 4 to 5 dozen cookies

Oven: 350°F   Bake Time: 10-15 min.

🖺 Passover Recipe

✍ This recipe appeared in the Sentinel some years ago as everyone was asking for the recipe. Try it throughout the year!

✓ Brown sugar may be used instead of regular sugar.

COOKIES

Toll House Cookies (D or P)

Shirley Rutkovitz

2 1/2 cups flour
1 teaspoon baking soda
1 teaspoon salt (if desired)
1 cup butter or margarine (at room temperature)
3/4 cup granulated sugar
3/4 cup firmly packed brown sugar
1 teaspoon vanilla extract
2 eggs
1 bag (12 oz.) semi-sweet or milk chocolate chips
1 cup chopped nuts

1. Preheat oven to 375°F.
2. Combine flour, baking soda and salt. Set aside.
3. In a large bowl, combine butter or margarine, sugars and vanilla. Beat until creamy.
4. Beat in eggs. Add flour mixture. Blend.
5. Stir in chocolate chips and nuts. Drop by rounded teaspoonsful onto greased cookie sheets.
6. Bake at 375°F for 10 to 12 minutes.

Makes about 4 dozen

Oven: 375°F   Bake Time: 10-12 min.

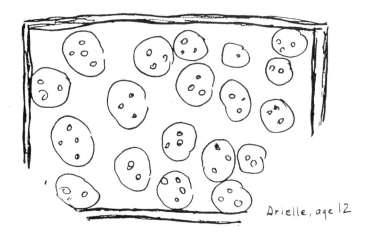

Arielle, age 12

Cake Mix Cookies (P)

Linda Platshon

1 package (18.5 oz.) cake mix of your choice
2 eggs
1/4 cup vegetable oil
1/2 to 1 teaspoon flavoring extract (vanilla, almond,
    lemon, etc.)
1 cup chocolate chips
chopped nuts or raisins, optional

1.   Combine half of the cake mix with the eggs, oil and
    extract. Mix until smooth.
2.   Stir in remaining cake mix and/or chocolate chips, nuts,
    and raisins.
3.   Drop by teaspoonfuls, about 2 inches apart, on ungreased
    cookie sheet. Bake at 375°F for 10 to 12 minutes. Centers
    will be soft. Allow to cool slightly before removing from
    cookie sheet.

Makes about 4 dozen

Oven: 375°F   Bake Time: 10-12 min.

✓These take 10 minutes to prepare and 12 minutes to bake.

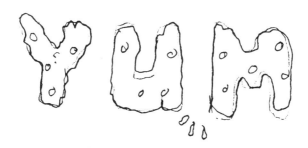

Sam, age 12

Nut Puffs (P)

Ethel Jaffe

1/2 cup margarine
2 Tablespoons sugar
1 teaspoon vanilla
1 cup finely chopped walnuts
1 cup sifted cake flour

powdered sugar

1. Cream margarine and sugar. Add vanilla and nuts.
2. Stir in flour and mix well.
3. Roll into 1-inch balls (about the size of large marbles).
4. Place on greased cookie sheet in slow oven (not over 300°F) for about 45 minutes. Roll in powdered sugar while hot and again when cool.

Makes about 20 puffs

Oven: 300°F   Bake Time: 45 min.

✐This is an international cookie! This popular recipe is sometimes çalled Russian Butter Balls— and is similar to Mexican Wedding Cakes.

Arielle, age 12

Lemon Poppy Seed Cookies (D)

Tinia Merkin

2 cups flour
1/2 teaspoon baking soda
2 teaspoons freshly grated lemon zest
2 Tablespoons poppy seeds
3/4 cup salted butter
1 cup sugar
2 eggs
1 1/2 teaspoons lemon extract

1. In medium bowl combine flour, baking soda, lemon zest and poppy seeds. Mix well with wire whisk. Set aside.
2. In a large bowl, cream butter and sugar with electric mixer at medium speed until mixture forms a grainy paste. Scrape down sides of bowl.
3. Add eggs and lemon extract. Beat at medium speed until light and fluffy.
4. Add flour mixture. Mix until combined.
5. Drop by tablespoon onto ungreased cookie sheet, 2 inches apart.
6. Bake at 300°F for 23 minutes.

Makes about 30 cookies

Oven : 300°F   Bake Time: 23 min.

Anna, age 12

Mom's Feather-Weight Cookies (P)

Linda Platshon

3 eggs
1 teaspoon almond extract
1/2 cup sugar
1 cup flour
1 teaspoon baking powder

flour

1. In a large bowl beat eggs and almond extract until frothy.
2. Add sugar, flour and baking powder. Mix well.
3. Use a small sieve (like a coffee strainer) to sprinkle a very light layer of flour on cookie sheet. Do not use too much flour as it will leave the cookies with floured bottoms.
4. Drop a heaping teaspoon of batter onto floured pan, about 2-inches apart as cookies will spread. The cookie batter is softer than most cookie dough. The batter will spread on the cookie sheet after it is placed, forming almost prefect circular cookies.
5. Bake at 350°F for 15 to 20 minutes until lightly browned at edges. Remove immediately to rack to cool. After cooling, excess flour on the bottoms can be brushed off.

Makes about 30 cookies

Oven: 350°F   Bake Time: 15 to 20 min.

✍Very airy, light delicate cookies. Crisp with a "sponge cake" texture. Very easy to make and uses no oil or shortening.

✓Vanilla, lemon or orange extract may be substituted for almond.

Selma's Brownies (D or P)

Linda Platshon

1/2 pound butter or margarine
4 squares (1 oz. each) unsweetened chocolate
2 cups sugar
4 eggs, slightly beaten
2 teaspoons vanilla
1 cup flour
walnuts, optional

1. Melt margarine and chocolate in top of double boiler or in microwave oven at low. Cool.
2. Mix in sugar. Add eggs and vanilla. Mix well.
3. Mix in flour. Pour into lightly greased 13x9-inch pan (or 2, 8-inch square pans). Sprinkle nuts on top if desired.
4. Bake at 350°F for 20 minutes. Cool before cutting.

Makes 12-16 pieces

Oven: 350°F   Bake Time: 20 min.

▤For Passover substitute flour with 3/4 cup potato starch and 1/4 cup matzo cake flour. Brownies will be very moist and fudgy.

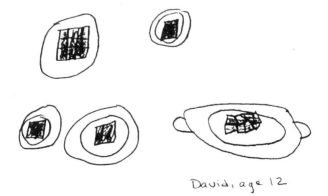

David, age 12

Four-Layer Squares (D)

Sharon Honig-Bear

First Layer (brownie base)
1 brownie recipe prepared (either use a box mix or your
    own recipe)
1/2 to 1 cup chopped nuts

Second Layer (extra "treat" layer)
2 cups graham cracker crumbs
1 cup chocolate chips
1 can (14 oz.) sweetened condensed milk
1/2 cup chopped nuts

Third Layer (butter cream layer)
6 Tablespoons butter
1 teaspoon vanilla
3 cups powdered sugar
3 Tablespoons milk

Fourth Layer (bitter chocolate glaze)
3 ounces bitter chocolate
3 Tablespoons butter

1. *First Layer:* Add nuts to prepared brownie batter. Spread
    brownie mixture in a greased 16x11-inch cookie sheet
    with sides. Freeze while preparing next layer.
2. *Second Layer:* Mix with fork graham crumbs, chocolate
    chips, condensed milk and nuts. The mixture is thick and
    sticky, using a fork helps. Drop mixture in small pieces
    dotting the top of the frozen brownies, then spread to
    completely cover.
3. Bake at 350°F for 30 minutes. Watch that the ends don't
    get too dry or brown. Cool thoroughly.
4. *Third Layer:* In food processor, combine butter, vanilla,
    sugar and milk until smooth. Spread over cooled layers.
5. *Fourth Layer:* Melt chocolate and butter together
    (microwave works fine). Drizzle glaze over existing three
    layers.

COOKIES

6.   Refrigerate (even freeze partially) before cutting into squares. This is a rich recipe and can make 20 to 50 pieces, depending on size cut.

Makes 20-50 squares

Oven 350°F   Bake Time: 30 min.

✍They're always a hit at Temple Sinai's bake sales. The recipe makes a large quantity...which makes the different steps worth the effort!

Lemon Squares (D or P)

Adrienne Tropp

2 cups and 1/4 cup flour
1/2 cup sifted powdered sugar
1 cup butter or margarine, melted
4 eggs
2 cups sugar
1/3 cup lemon juice
1/2 teaspoon baking powder
garnish with powdered sugar

1.   In large bowl combine 2 cups flour and powdered sugar.
2.   Mix in butter. Press mixture into 13x9x2-inch baking pan. Bake at 350°F for 20 minutes. Set aside.
3.   In same, now empty bowl, beat eggs. Then beat in sugar and lemon juice.
4.   Combine 1/4 cup flour and baking powder. Stir into egg mixture. Pour over baked crust. Bake at 350°F for 25 minutes or until set and browned. Cool.
5.   Sift powdered sugar over. Cut into 1-inch squares.

Makes about 10 dozen

Oven: 350°F   Bake Time: 45 min.

Rocky Road Squares (D)

Linda Kutten

1 package (18 oz.) devils food cake mix
1/3 cup butter, melted
1/4 cup packed brown sugar
1/3 cup water
2 eggs
1 cup chopped walnuts
1 bag (oz.) miniature marshmallows
1 tub (16 oz.) chocolate ready-to-spread frosting

1. Mix together until smooth cake mix, butter, brown sugar, water and eggs.
2. Stir in walnuts.
3. Spread into a greased and floured 9x13-inch pan. Bake in 350°F oven for 20 minutes.
4. Sprinkle marshmallows over top. Return to oven for 10 to 15 minutes until marshmallows are puffed and golden.
5. Remove cover and foil top from frosting tub. Heat frosting in microwave oven for 1 minute. Drizzle thinned frosting over marshmallows. Cool.

Makes 35 squares

Oven: 350°F   Bake Time: 30 - 35 min.

✓Use a plastic disposable knife to cut the squares for less sticking when cutting.

CAKES

Honey Chiffon Cake (P)

Helene Paris

4 eggs, separated
1 cup sugar
1 cup honey
1 cup oil
3 1/2 cups flour
1/2 teaspoon salt
2 teaspoons baking soda
2 teaspoons baking powder
1 teaspoon cinnamon
1 teaspoon nutmeg
1 teaspoon ground cloves
1 cup strong coffee
1/4 to 1/2 cup raisins (optional)

1. Beat egg whites until stiff and set aside.
2. In a large mixing bowl, beat egg yolks until fluffy. Gradually add sugar and beat well. Beat in honey and oil.
3. Mix together all dry ingredients and add alternately with coffee to egg yolk mixture.
4. Add raisins if desired.
5. Pour into 13x9-inch greased pan. Bake at 300°F for 1 hour.

Makes 13x9-inch cake

Oven: 300°F   Bake Time: 1 hour

HONEY CAKE is *lekah* in Yiddish. Honey cake is traditionally served at Rosh Hashanah.

Honey Bundt Cake (D or P)

Laura Ashkin

1/2 cup butter or margarine
1 cup sugar
1 cup honey
3 eggs
1 cup warm strong black coffee
3 cups flour
1 teaspoon baking soda
3 teaspoons baking powder
2 teaspoons cinnamon
2 teaspoons ground ginger
1/2 teaspoon nutmeg
1/2 teaspoon cloves
1/2 teaspoon allspice
1 cup walnuts, chopped

Icing
Juice of one lemon
Quarter stick (2 oz.) soft margarine, cut up
Powdered sugar

1. In the processor, first put in the shortening and sugar and process until it's smooth. It'll be sort of a ball.
2. Add the honey, eggs and coffee, making a thin batter.
3. Next put in the 3 cups of flour and arrange all the other teaspoons of spices and baking soda/powder rather evenly on top of the flour (so you won't end up inadvertently with clumps of cinnamon , etc. in one place). Process for a few short bursts just until it's all mixed.
4. Put in the nuts and process for a few more short bursts.
5. Profusely grease Bundt pan with margarine and then dust with flour. Or use non-stick pan. Pour batter into pan. Bake in preheated 350°F oven for about 45 minutes or until a toothpick comes out clean. Cool.
6. *For the icing*: Mix in a mixer lemon juice and butter. Beat

CAKES

in sugar to desired consistency. Drizzle icing artistically from the top over the cooled cake.

Makes 1 bundt cake

Oven: 350°F   Bake Time: 45 min.

✍This cake has been a popular at the Temple Sinai Rosh Hashanah Outdoor Service for years.

✓The recipe is modified for the food processor.

✓The icing is on the runny side. It may appear curdled, but never mind. It tastes great anyway. Ice the cake a day ahead to soak in the taste and moisten the cake.

Carly age 12

Mary's Honey Loaf Cake (P)

Mary Aaronson

4 eggs
1 cup sugar
1 cup packed brown sugar
6 Tablespoons oil
16 ounces honey
1 cup warm dark coffee
1 orange, juice and grated zest
5 1/2 cups flour
2 teaspoons baking soda
2 teaspoons baking powder
2 teaspoons cinnamon
2 teaspoons allspice
2 cup walnuts, chopped

10-12 walnut halves

1. Beat eggs well. Mix in sugars, oil, honey, coffee, orange juice and orange zest.
2. Sift together flour, baking soda, baking powder, cinnamon, and allspice. Add a little at a time to sugar mixture. Mixing well after each addition.
3. Stir in chopped walnuts.
4. Pour into two greased 9x5-inch loaf pans. Decorate top with walnut halves. Bake at 325°F for 1 hour.

Makes 2 loaf cakes

Oven Temp: 325 °F   Bake Time: 1 hour

George's Honey Cake (P)

George Small, Major U.S. Army, Retired

3 eggs
1 cup sugar
2 Tablespoons vegetable oil
3 1/2 cups flour
2 teaspoons baking powder
1 teaspoon baking soda
1/2 teaspoon salt
1/2 teaspoon ground ginger
1/2 teaspoon nutmeg
1 teaspoon cinnamon
1/4 teaspoon ground cloves
1 cup honey
1 cup warm coffee
1 1/2 cups slivered almonds

1. In small bowl, beat eggs, sugar and oil until smooth.
2. Combine in large bowl flour, baking powder, baking soda, salt, ginger, nutmeg, cinnamon, and cloves. Add egg mixture. Stir until batter becomes stiff.
3. Add honey and warm coffee. Stir. When batter mixes easily add almonds.
4. Pour into a non-stick 13x9x2-inch baking pan. Bake at 325°F for 1 hour.
5. Cool in pan. Wrap with plastic wrap to prevent loss of moisture and refrigerate.

Makes 13x9-inch cake

Oven: 325°F   Bake Time: 1 hour

✍After the American forces in Bataan surrendered, we were forced to make the "Bataan Death March" to a Japanese prisoner of war camp. There were three and a half years of starvation and abuse before liberation. When I returned home, one of my first requests was for my mother's honey cake.

Applesauce Spice Cake (P)

Julie Stage

1 egg
1 cup sugar
1/2 cup oil
1/4 teaspoon salt
1 teaspoon cinnamon
1 teaspoon cloves
1 teaspoon allspice
1 1/3 cups applesauce
1 cup pecans
1 cup raisins
2 1/2 cups flour
3/4 teaspoon baking powder

1. Combine egg, sugar, oil and salt. Add spices. Mix well.
2. Add applesauce, pecans and raisins. Mix well.
3. Sift together flour and baking powder. Stir into above mixture.
4. Pour into greased or sprayed 13x9-inch pan. Bake at 300°F for 1 hour.

Makes 13x9-inch cake

Oven: 300°F   Bake Time: 1 hour

✍This recipe from my mother, Louise Halprin Wilson.

✓This cake is so moist, it needs no frosting. A great alternative to the traditional honey cake.

Applesauce Cinnamon Cake (P)

Elizabeth Kempler

1 cup vegetable shortening
2 cups brown sugar
2 eggs
3 cups flour
2 teaspoons baking soda
1 teaspoon salt
2 cups applesauce
2 teaspoons cinnamon
Juice of one lemon
1 cup raisins, optional
1/2 cup chopped walnuts, optional

1. Cream shortening, sugar and eggs until light and fluffy.
2. Sift flour, soda and salt.
3. Mix applesauce with cinnamon and lemon juice.
4. To egg mixture, add flour mixture alternately with applesauce mixture, beating well after each addition. If you desire, add raisins and walnuts.
5. Pour into two greased and lightly floured 9x5-inch loaf pans.
6. Bake at 350°F for about one hour or until toothpick inserted in center comes out clean.

Makes 2 loaves

Oven: 350°F   Bake Time: 1 hour

Apple Cake (P)

Nancy Simkin, Jewish Fest Recipe

6 large apples, preferably Granny Smiths
3 teaspoons cinnamon
3 teaspoons sugar
1 cup vegetable oil
4 eggs
2 1/2 cups sugar
3 cups flour
3 teaspoons baking powder
1/2 teaspoon salt
1/3 cup orange juice
2 1/2 teaspoons vanilla

1. Peel and core apples. Slice thinly.
2. Combine apple slices, cinnamon and sugar. Set aside.
3. Place remaining ingredients into a large bowl in the order given. Mix well. Batter will be stiff.
4. Spread a third of the batter into greased and floured large tube cake or Bundt pan. Layer a third of the apples. Spread half of the remaining batter over apples; layer half of remaining apples, top with remaining batter, then apple slices.
5. Bake at 350°F for 60 minutes. Turn oven down to 325°F and bake another 60 minutes. If top is turning too dark, cover lightly with foil.
6. Cool on rack for 10 minutes. Carefully remove from pan, apple side up. You may need another set of hands to help lift the cake out and onto a cooling rack. Cool completely.

Makes 12 servings

Oven: 350°F & 325°F   Bake Time: 2 hours

✓Granny Smith apples hold their shape in baking.

CAKES

Rosh Hashanah Apple Cake (P)

Julie Stage

2 cups sugar
1/2 cup oil
2 eggs
2 cups flour
2 teaspoons baking soda
1 teaspoon salt
2 teaspoons cinnamon
1 teaspoon nutmeg
4 cups diced tart apples

1. Prepare a 13x9-inch pan by spraying with vegetable cooking spray. Preheat oven to 350°F.
2. Combine sugar, oil and eggs. Add remaining ingredients, mix well. Bake at 350°F for 1 hour. Let cool before cutting.

Makes 13x9-inch cake

Oven: 350°F   Bake Time: 1 hour

✓This is a very moist cake and needs no frosting. Filled with diced apples!

✓You can cut the fat in half, if in place of 1/2 cup oil you use 1/4 cup applesauce and 1/4 cup oil. There are no adjustments needed for altitude.

CAKES

Carrot Cake (D)

Barbara Weinberg

Cake Batter
2 cups sifted flour
2 teaspoons baking powder
1 1/2 teaspoons baking soda
1 teaspoon salt
2 1/2 teaspoons cinnamon
2 cups sugar
1 1/2 cups oil
4 large eggs
2 3/4 cups coarsely grated carrots
1 can (8 oz.) crushed pineapple (drained)
3/4 cup chopped walnuts or pecans
1 cup shredded sweetened coconut

Cream Cheese Frosting
1/2 cup butter or margarine
1 package (8 oz.) cream cheese
1 1/2 teaspoons vanilla
1 package (1pound) powdered sugar
1 teaspoon milk

1. *For cake*: Sift together flour, baking powder, baking soda, salt, and cinnamon.
2. In a large bowl, mix sugar, oil, and eggs.
3. Add flour mixture a little at a time, mixing well after each addition.
4. Add carrots, pineapple, nuts, and coconut. Blend thoroughly.
5. Turn into either 3 greased and floured 8-inch round cake pans OR one 13x9-inch, deep, greased and floured cake pan.
6. Bake at 350°F for 30 to 40 minutes. If removing cake from pan, let cool for about ten minutes before removal. Cool completely.

CAKES

7. *For frosting*: Soften butter and cream cheese. Cream together with vanilla.
8. Sift in powdered sugar and blend well. (Start with about half a pound powdered sugar and add more to taste, a pound may be too sweet.) If too thick, add milk to thin frosting. Frost cooled cake.

Makes 3-layered cake or13x9-inch cake

Oven: 350°F   Bake Time: 40 min.

✍This Carrot Cake is absolutely delicious!

✓Carrot cake will keep well in refrigerator for at least a week.

Adam, age 12

Lazy Daisy Oatmeal Cake (D)

Patricia Blanchard

1 1/4 cups boiling water
1 cup quick or old fashioned oats, uncooked
1/2 cup butter or margarine, softened
1 cup granulated sugar
1 cup firmly packed brown sugar
1 teaspoon vanilla
2 eggs
1 1/2 cups sifted flour
1 teaspoon baking soda
1/2 teaspoon salt
3/4 teaspoon cinnamon
1/2 teaspoon nutmeg

Frosting
1/4 cup butter or margarine, melted
1/2 cup firmly packed brown sugar
3 Tablespoons half & half milk
1/3 cup chopped nuts
3/4 cup shredded or flaked coconut

1. Pour boiling water over oats. Cover and let stand 20 minutes.
2. Beat butter until creamy. Gradually beat in sugars. Beat until light and fluffy. Blend in vanilla and eggs. Add oat mixture. Mix well.
3. Sift together flour, baking soda, salt, cinnamon and nutmeg. Add to butter mixture and mix well. Pour into well greased and floured 9-inch square pan. Bake in preheated 350°F oven for 50 to 55 minutes. Do not remove cake from pan.
4. *For Frosting*: Combine all frosting ingredients. Spread evenly over cake. Broil until frosting becomes bubbly. Serve warm or cold.

Makes 9-inch square cake Oven: 350°F Bake Time: 55 min.

Passover Carrot Walnut Sponge Cake (P)

Elizabeth Kempler

8 eggs, separated
1 1/2 cups sugar
1 cup matzo cake meal
1 cup grated carrots, patted dry
Juice of 1/2 lemon and grated zest
Juice of one orange
1 cup chopped walnuts

1. Preheat oven to 350°F.
2. Beat egg whites until forming stiff peaks. Set aside.
3. Beat egg yolks with sugar until light yellow.
3. Add cake meal, carrots, lemon juice and zest, and orange juice. Set aside.
4. Gently fold beaten whites into cake mixture, adding walnuts as you fold. Pour into 10-inch tube pan and bake at 350°F for 45 minutes.

Makes 1 tube cake

Oven: 350°F   Bake Time: 45 min.

▤This pareve (no dairy) cake is excellent for a Seder.

✓The recipe also works well as cupcakes: follow the recipe but omit carrots. Bake in greased cupcake tins at 350°F for 25 minutes.

Martha Gould's English Trifle (D)

Martha Gould

Pastry cream
5 egg yolks
2/3 cup sugar
1/3 cup flour
dash of salt
2 cups milk
1 Tablespoon butter
1 1/2 teaspoons vanilla

2/3 cup sherry wine
1/3 cup brandy
1 Pound cake, sliced
raspberry jam (or boysenberry or strawberry)
lady fingers

Whipped Cream
heavy whipping cream, cold
sugar
vanilla

1. *For Pastry cream*: Beat egg yolks well. Mix in sugar, flour and salt. Beat well. Heat milk in saucepan. Gradually beat hot milk into egg mixture. Pour mixture back into saucepan. Cook and stir until thickened. Remove from heat add butter and vanilla. Let cool.
2. Combine sherry and brandy.
3. In trifle bowl or deep dish, layer pound cake and pour some sherry-brandy mixture over. Spread jam, followed by lady fingers moistened with sherry-brandy mixture. Top with pastry cream. Repeat as many layers as the bowl will hold.
4. Beat cold whipping cream until stiff. Fold in sugar and vanilla to taste. Spread over trifle. Chill until ready to serve.

Makes 1 large bowl of trifle

✓ If you so wish, you can add candied cherries or fruit or whatever moves you. As far as I am concerned the basic trifle does it, especially when the cake and lady fingers are well soaked (or crocked).

Sour Cream Pound Cake (D)

Linda Platshon

>3 cups flour
>1/4 teaspoon baking soda
>2 sticks butter or margarine (1/2 pound)
>3 cups sugar
>6 eggs
>1 cup sour cream
>1 teaspoon vanilla

1. Sift flour 2 times. Add baking soda and sift again. Set aside.
2. Beat together butter and sugar until fluffy.
3. Add eggs one at a time, beating well after each egg.
4. Stir in sour cream, flour mixture and vanilla.
5. Pour into greased 10-inch tube or Bundt pan.
6. Bake 325°F for 1 hour 30 minutes. Cool in pan.

Makes 1 tube cake

Oven: 325°F   Bake Time: 1 hr 30 min.

Opera Torte (D)

Adrienne Tropp

Hazelnut Sponge Cake
3 egg whites
1 Tablespoon sugar
2/3 cup powdered sugar
3 Tablespoons flour
1/2 cup plus 1/8 rounded cup ground hazelnuts, toasted
3 eggs
1 Tablespoon butter, melted and cooled

Chocolate Ganache
1/2 cup heavy whipping cream
7 ounces bittersweet chocolate
1/4 cup sugar

Coffee Syrup
1 Tablespoon instant coffee crystals
1 Tablespoon sugar
1/2 cup water

Butter cream
2 Tablespoons water
2/3 cup sugar
2 egg whites
2/3 cup unsalted butter, cut in chunks
a bit of the coffee syrup

1. *For Hazelnut Sponge Cake*: Preheat oven to 425°F. In a small bowl beat egg whites until stiff. Beat in 1 Tablespoon sugar until stiff peaks form. Set aside. In a large bowl mix together powdered sugar, flour and hazelnuts. Add eggs and beat until pale, about 3 minutes. Fold in butter. Fold in a third of the beaten whites. Then carefully fold in the remaining beaten whites. Line 16x11-inch jelly roll pan with parchment paper. Grease paper.

Spread batter evenly in pan. Bake at 425°F for 6 to 7 minutes or until golden, Turn out onto wire rack. Remove paper. Cool.

2. *Chocolate Ganache*: In a small saucepan heat cream to boil. Remove from heat. Add chocolate and sugar. Let sit 2 to 3 minutes. Then stir until chocolate is melted. Cool.

3. *Coffee Syrup*: In a small saucepan combine coffee crystals, sugar and water. Boil for 5 minutes. Cool.

4. *Butter cream*: In a small saucepan combine water and sugar. Bring to softball stage (240°F), until liquid can be poured. Beat egg whites until frothy. Drizzle sugar syrup into bowl while beating on high. Keep beating until whites are very stiff and mixture has cooled. On medium speed, beat in chunks of butter, one at a time. Once mixture has come together, add a bit of coffee syrup, just enough so the butter cream has a hint of coffee taste.

5. *Assembling*: Cut cake crosswise into 3 pieces. Brush all three with coffee syrup. Place one piece on serving plate. Spread with half of butter cream. Cover with second layer. Spread with half of the ganache. Cover with the last layer. Top with butter cream. Smooth the top and refrigerate until butter cream is firmly set.

6. *Finishing*: Warm the remaining ganache until it is of spreading consistency. Spread over top of refrigerated firmly set cake. Return to refrigerator to set ganache.

7. *Serving*: Cut into slices and serve. A serrated knife works well

Makes 1, 11x7-inch torte (slice into thin slices as it is rich)

Oven: 425°F   Bake Time: 7 min.

Refrigerate: Several hours

Famous Weinberg Chocolate Matzo (D or P)

Barbara Weinberg

1 1/2 pounds (24 oz.) semi-sweet chocolate chips
2 to 3 Tablespoons butter or margarine

8 matzo squares
pot of boiling water

1. Melt chocolate chips and butter together in top of double boiler. Keep warm.
2. Remove matzo from box by cutting off one large square side of box. Line inside of box with aluminum foil. The box is your "baking pan" and storage box. Set aside extra matzo for other projects.
3. One at a time, run matzo under warm water then steam on a cake rack over boiling water for 1 to 2 minutes, until soft but not soggy.
4. Carefully place one softened matzo in foil-lined box and drizzle heavily with one-eighth of the melted chocolate. Repeat layering with all 8 matzo, ending with chocolate. Refrigerate until ready to eat.
5. Cut into 25 squares, 8 layers deep, with a wet knife.

Makes 25 servings

▤Passover Recipe

✍From Harry Weinberg's mother who called it Kalte Schnautze or "cold nose" in German.

▤An excuse for eating chocolate at Passover.

✓For ease in slicing, stack matzo with grooves running in the same direction.

✓ For a fancy look, scatter top layer with slivered nuts while chocolate is warm and wet.

CAKES

Layered Matzo Cake (P)

Nancy Daum

Chocolate mixture
8 ounces semi-sweet chocolate chips
1 Tablespoon margarine
8 ounces apricot jam or orange marmalade
2 eggs
2 Tablespoons Kahlua coffee liqueur

1 cup Kahlua coffee liqueur
10 matzos
chopped nuts

1. Melt the chocolate, margarine and jam in microwave oven.
2. Add eggs and beat until mixture is thick.
3. Add 2 Tablespoons coffee liqueur & continue to beat until mixture thickens again.
4. Pour 1 cup coffee liqueur into a large shallow dish. Dip the matzos in the liqueur one at a time just to moisten.
5. Place one matzo on a cake plate and coat with a layer of chocolate mixture Top with another moistened matzo and more chocolate until all matzos are used.
6. Use remaining chocolate to frost sides. Decorate with nuts and let stand at room temperature to set before serving.

Makes 1 layered matzo cake

▤Passover Recipe

✍My family is rich in traditional Jewish cooking going back over 100 years. Betty (Hal's sister) gathered these recipes from "Mom" (Molly Daum) and Hal & Betty. And we chose a few for you to use in your Temple cookbook. We didn't include some recipes that say "ask Hal" or "ask Betty!"

Passover Wine Cake (P)

Adrienne Tropp

2/3 cup matzo cake meal
1/3 cup potato starch
1 teaspoon cinnamon
1/2 teaspoon ground ginger
pinch salt
9 large eggs, separated
1 1/2 cups sugar
3/4 cups ground walnuts
1/4 cup sweet red wine

1. Preheat oven to 350°F.
2. Stir together cake meal, potato starch, cinnamon, ginger and salt. Set aside.
3. Beat egg whites until stiff peaks form but not dry.
4. In a large bowl, beat egg yolks until foamy. Gradually beat in sugar. Then gradually beat in cake meal mixture.
5. Mix together walnuts and wine. Fold into egg yolk mixture.
6. Fold beaten egg whites into egg yolk mixture. Pour into greased and floured 10-inch tube pan. Bake at 350°F for 60 minutes.

Makes 8 servings

Oven: 350°F   Bake Time: 60 min.

▤Passover Recipe

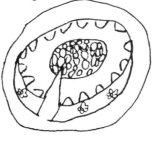

Alex, age 12

Passover Sponge Cake (P)

Shirley Rutkovitz

6 eggs, separated
1/4 teaspoon salt, if desired
1 1/3 cups sugar
1 whole egg
1/4 cup hot water
1 lemon, grated zest and juice
1/2 cup potato starch
1/2 cup matzo cake meal

1. Preheat oven to 350°F. Place waxed paper in bottom of 10-inch tube pan.
2. Beat egg whites until stiff. Add salt, if desired. Set aside.
3. Beat egg yolks and sugar together until light.
4. Add whole egg, hot water, lemon zest and juice. Set aside.
5. Sift together potato starch and cake meal. Stir into egg mixture.
6. Fold beaten egg whites into egg yolk mixture.
7. Pour into waxed paper-lined tube pan. Bake at 350°F for 1 hour or until top is brown and cracked. Invert and let cool before taking out of pan.

Makes 8 to 10 servings

Oven: 350°F   Bake Time: 1 hour

▤Passover Recipe

✐Recipe from my mother, Anne Lutzker.

✓Chopped nuts may be folded into batter before pouring into tube pan.

Farfel Cupcakes (D)

Lori Lacey

12 eggs
1 1/2 cups sugar
1 cup butter, melted
1 teaspoon cinnamon
1 quart (4 cups) milk
2 boxes (16 oz each) matzo farfel
1 box (15 oz.) seedless raisins
1 box (15 oz.) golden raisins
1 pound dried seedless prunes, cut up
1 pound dried apricots, cut up
1/2 pound candied pineapple, cut up
1/2 pound candied cherries, cut up
dates, optional
chocolate chips, if desired

1. Beat eggs well. Add sugar. Continue to beat well.
2. Beat in melted butter. Mix cinnamon and milk in thoroughly.
3. Add farfel. Mix well. Add remaining ingredients. Mix thoroughly.
4. Grease cupcake tins generously. Fill to 1/4-inch from top. Bake at 350°F for 35 minutes or until light brown.
5. Remove from pans immediately. Use a knife to loosen cupcakes from pan.

Makes about 80 cupcakes

Oven: 350°F   Bake Time: 35 min.

▤Passover Recipe

✓ This is a large recipe but can be easily halved or quartered. Be sure to grease the cups generously (even non-stick pans) and remove the cupcakes from the pan immediately upon removal from the oven otherwise the cupcakes will not come out in one piece.

Easy Cheese Cupcakes (D)

Linda Platshon

12 vanilla wafers
cupcake foil liners
2 packages (8 oz. each) cream cheese, softened
1 teaspoon vanilla
1/2 cup sugar
2 eggs

1. Place one vanilla wafer in each foil liner in muffin pan.
2. Mix cream cheese, vanilla, and sugar on medium speed until well blended.
3. Add eggs. Mix well.
4. Pour over wafers, filling 3/4 full.
5. Bake at 325°F for 25 minutes.
6. Remove from pan when cool. Chill.
7. To serve: Top with fruit preserves, nuts or chocolate.

Makes: 12 cheese cupcakes

Oven: 325°F   Bake Time: 25 min.

Joe, age 12

Low-Fat Cheesecake (D)

Linda Platshon

Linda Platshon

Grape-Nuts® pie crust
1 1/2 cups grape-nuts cereal
1/4 cup butter
sugar, if desired

Filling
2 cups nonfat cottage cheese
1/4 cup nonfat plain yogurt
1 egg white
1/4 cup frozen orange juice concentrate, thawed
1/3 cup frozen apple juice concentrate, thawed
1 teaspoon vanilla

Your choice of fresh fruit toppings

1. *For Crust*: Preheat oven to 350°F. In food processor or blender combine cereal, butter and sugar to taste until fine. Press mixture firmly on bottom and sides of 8-inch pie pan. Bake at 375°F for 15 minutes. Cool.
2. *For Filling*: In a blender or food processor, blend cottage cheese till smooth. Add yogurt, egg white, orange juice concentrate, apple juice concentrate and vanilla. Blend till smooth.
3. Pour into pie crust. Bake at 350°F for 20 minutes. Chill and serve with your choice of fresh fruit toppings (sliced strawberries, blueberries or cherries).

Makes 8-inch pie

Oven: 350°F   Bake Time: 35 minutes

New York Cheesecake (D)

Lynne Daus, Jewish Fest recipe

8 ounces (1 cup) butter
1 package (13.5 oz.) graham cracker crumbs
18 ounces cream cheese
2 cups sour cream
2 eggs
1 cup sugar
1 teaspoon vanilla
1/2 teaspoon lemon juice
Cherry pie filling

1. Melt butter. Stir in graham cracker crumbs. Pat into 9-inch spring-form cake pan.
2. In food processor, blend cream cheese and sour cream until smooth. Pour contents into mixing bowl. Mix in eggs, sugar, vanilla and lemon juice.
3. Pour into graham cracker crumb lined pan. Bake in 350°F oven for 30 to 35 minutes until not too jiggly. Turn oven off, open door; leave cake in oven for another hour.
4. Pour cherry topping over all. Or refrigerate until ready to eat.

Makes 9-inch cheesecake

Oven: 350°F   Bake Time: 30-35 min.

✓To freeze, take cheesecake out of pan and place on cardboard. Freeze 1 hour then wrap.

✓For Mini cheesecakes: Line muffin tins with foil liners with paper liner next to cheesecake. Press about 2 tablespoons of crumb mixture in each muffin liner. Pour in cheesecake mixture till almost full. Bake in 350°F oven for 25 minutes. Makes 24 cupcheesecakes.

Pumpkin Cheesecake (D)

Linda Kutten

1 box (16 oz.) gingersnaps, finely crushed
1/2 cup butter
4 packages (8 oz. each) cream cheese, softened
1 cup packed brown sugar
3/4 cup plus 1 Tablespoon sugar
1/4 cup flour
2 teaspoons cinnamon
1 teaspoon ginger
1/2 teaspoon cloves
1/4 teaspoon allspice
5 eggs
1 can (16 oz.) pumpkin

1. Combine gingersnaps and butter (the food processor works great in crushing the gingersnaps). Reserve 1 cup of crumbs. Press remaining into bottom of buttered 9-inch springform pan or a 9x13-inch metal pan.
2. Beat cream cheese until smooth. Gradually beat in until well blended the sugar, flour, cinnamon, ginger, cloves, and allspice.
3. On Low beat in eggs, one at a time, beating just until blended. Add pumpkin and beat until well mixed.
4. Pour into gingersnap crust-lined pan. Sprinkle reserved cup of crumbs over top. Bake at 325°F for 1 hour 20 minutes to 1 hour 30 minutes, until a knife inserted near the center comes out clean and the center has puffed up slightly. Remove from oven. Cool to room temperature on wire rack. Cover. Refrigerate overnight to set.

Makes 9-inch cheesecake

Oven: 325°F   Bake Time: 1 hr. 20 min. to 1 hr. 30 min.

DESSERTS

Carisse's Strudel (D)

Carisse Gafni

2 sticks (8 oz.) margarine or butter, softened
1 carton (8 oz.) sour cream
2 cups flour

fruit jam of your liking
chopped walnuts
shredded coconut

1. Mix together margarine, sour cream and flour. Form into 2 balls. Cover. Refrigerate at least 2 hours.
2. Roll a ball out on floured board to about 12x18-inches. Spread with jam to about 1 to 1 1/2-inches from the ends. Cover jam with walnuts and coconut. Fold a third of the edge over to cover the middle third. The fold the remaining third over the other two, so there are 3 layers. Pinch to close ends. Place on cookie sheet. Repeat with the second ball
3. Bake at 375°F for 45 minutes.

Makes 2 strudels

Refrigerate 2 hours   Oven: 375°F   Bake Time: 45 min.

▤STRUDEL is a baked pastry with a very flaky crust. The pastry is rolled very thin (sometimes filo dough is substituted), a filling is spread/sprinkled over all then rolled up into a log and baked. The filling varies greatly from a sweet fruit and nuts to poppy seeds or cheese or cabbage (see the Cabbage Strudel recipe in the vegetable section).

Fruit Strudel (D)

Ethel Jaffe

Pearl's Cream Cheese Dough
1/2 pound butter, softened
1 package (8 oz.) cream cheese, softened
4 Tablespoons sugar
Pinch (1/8 teaspoon) salt
2 cups flour

Filling
Apricot-Pineapple Jam, or your favorite
Flaked coconut
Finely chopped walnuts

1. *For dough*: Cream butter and cream cheese. Add other ingredients, form into 3 or 4 balls, cover with plastic wrap and refrigerate overnight.
2. Remove dough from refrigerator about 15 minutes before using and roll blattle (sheet) thin.
3. Spread thinly rolled dough with a thin layer of jam.
4. Sprinkle with coconut and then with walnuts. Tuck ends in and roll up the dough. Place on greased baking sheets and bake at 350°F for about 40-45 minutes or until lightly brown. Cut immediately into slices.

Makes about 25 slices

Oven: 350°F   Bake Time: 40-45 min

✍This is a slightly sweetened version of Rugelach dough. The apricot- pineapple flavor is a favorite of the Jaffe family.

✓Refrigerating the dough overnight helps in rolling and flavoring.

Passover Strudel (P)

Linda Platshon

Dough
4 eggs
1/2 cup vegetable oil
2 cups matzo cake meal
1 cup potato starch
1/2 cup sugar
4 Tablespoons cold water
pinch of salt
Filling
1 pound chopped walnuts
2 large apples, grated
1 orange zest, grated
1 lemon zest, grated
2 Tablespoons matzo meal
1/4 cup sugar
1 Tablespoon cinnamon
preserves or jelly

Cinnamon-sugar mixture, if desired

1. *For dough*: Beat eggs and stir in all dough ingredients. Mix well and divide into 5 portions.
2. *For filling*: Mix together all filling ingredients except preserves. Divide into 5 portions.
3. *To Assemble*: Roll out one portion of dough between two sheets of waxed paper to about a 9-inch square. Remove top waxed paper. Spread one portion, a fifth, of the filling mix and preserves on top of rolled dough. Roll up and place on greased cookie sheet. Repeat for the remaining 4 portions. Cut halfway through strudels, making 8 slices. Sprinkle with cinnamon-sugar mixture. Bake at 350°F for 1 hour. As soon as removed from oven, complete slicing.

Makes 40 slices   Oven: 350°F   Bake Time: 1 hr.
▤Passover Recipe

Linda's Easy Strudel (P)

Linda Platshon

2 cups flour
2 eggs
1 cup vegetable shortening
1/2 cup water
pinch salt

1/4 cup margarine, melted
3/4 cup cinnamon-sugar mixture
1 1/2 cups raisins
1 1/2 cups apricot or blackberry jam, if desired

1. Mix together well flour, eggs, shortening, water and salt to make dough. Divide into 6 parts. Wrap and chill until ready to use.
2. For each portion, roll on floured board into a 9-inch square. Brush with melted margarine. Sprinkle with 2 Tablespoons cinnamon-sugar and 1/4 cup raisins. Spread 1/4 cup jam, if desired. Roll up like jelly roll. Place seam down on parchment lined cookie sheet. Slice diagonally through top only.
3. Bake at 400°F for 15 minutes. Then turn oven to 350°F and bake 30 to 40 minutes until brown.
4. Slice. Sprinkle with powdered sugar and serve.

Makes about 48 slices

Oven: 400°F & 350°F   Bake Time: 55 min.

✓Freezes well.

✓For other flavors, for each roll, brush with margarine and sprinkle with cinnamon-sugar as above but instead of raisins and jam: use 1 diced apple and 1/4 cup chopped pecans; use 1/4 cup blueberries and 1/4 cup chopped pecans; OR add 1/4 cup chopped pecans or walnuts and the jam.

DESSERTS

Nectarine Crisp (D)

Sharry Springmeyer

Streusel Topping
2/3 cup butter, softened
1/3 cup packed brown sugar
1/2 cup granulated sugar
1 1/3 cups flour
1/4 teaspoon baking powder
1/2 teaspoon ground cinnamon
3/4 cup chopped walnuts, lightly toasted

Filling
1 cup packed brown sugar
3 Tablespoons flour
6 cups unpeeled, sliced nectarines (or peaches, etc.)
1 Tablespoon vanilla
1 Tablespoon kirsch (cherry brandy)
1 Tablespoon lemon or orange zest

1. *For topping:* beat the butter and sugars in bowl of an electric mixer until light and fluffy. Add flour, baking powder and cinnamon. Mix well. Add walnuts and mix to combine. Loosely pack the mixture in a shallow container and freeze until firm.
2. *For filling:* lightly butter a 9x9-inch baking pan.
3. Mix together brown sugar and flour. Toss with the nectarines, vanilla, kirsch and zest. Spread evenly over the bottom of the buttered pan.
4. Preheat oven to 350°F.
5. Transfer the frozen streusel topping to the food processor container. Process until the size of small pebbles. Crumble over the nectarine filling.
6. Bake at 350°F for 35 minutes or until top is golden and bubbles appear at the sides. Serve warm with vanilla ice cream or whipped cream.

Makes 9 servings   Oven: 350°F   Bake Time: 35 min.

DESSERTS

Chocolate Soufflé Roll (D)

Adrienne Tropp

Roll
7 ounces dark semisweet chocolate
4 Tablespoons strong coffee
7 eggs, separated
1/4 cup and 1/2 cup sugar

Mocha Cream Filling
3 ounces semisweet chocolate
2 Tablespoons strong coffee
9 Tablespoons pareve margarine
3/4 cup very fine sugar (do not use granulated sugar)
2 eggs
2 Tablespoons cocoa

Whipped Cream Frosting
1 cup heavy cream
1 teaspoon vanilla or rum
2 teaspoons powdered sugar
Shaved chocolate

1. *For Roll:* Preheat oven to 350°F. Grease a 15x10-inch jelly roll pan. Line with waxed paper. Grease paper.
2. Melt chocolate in coffee in double boiler over hot water or in microwave oven, stirring frequently, until chocolate melts. Cool.
3. Beat egg whites until soft peaks form. Gradually beat in 1/4 cup sugar. Beat until stiff peaks form. Set aside.
4. In a large bowl, beat egg yolks and 1/2 cup sugar until fluffy and pale yellow in color. Beat in chocolate mixture. Fold in beaten egg whites. Spread onto prepared jelly roll pan. Bake at 350°F for 15 to 20 minutes or until roll is firm. Remove from oven and cool for 5 minutes. Then place a damp towel over the roll and cool completely at room temperature. The damp towel keeps the roll from

drying.

5. *For Mocha Filling:* Melt chocolate in coffee in top of double boiler over boiling water or in the microwave oven, stirring frequently, until chocolate is melted. Set aside to cool slightly. Beat together well margarine and sugar. Beat in chocolate mixture. Then beat in eggs until smooth and light.

6. *To Assemble:* Remove damp towel from roll. Sprinkle with 2 Tablespoons cocoa. Top with waxed paper. Turn over roll in pan so that the top is now resting on the cocoa and waxed paper. Remove pan and peel off waxed paper that the roll baked on. Spread with mocha filling. Carefully and quickly roll up lengthwise. The roll usually cracks a bit on rolling but the frosting will cover it. Cover and refrigerate until ready to serve. To serve frost with whipped cream frosting.

7. *For Whipped Cream Frosting:* Beat together heavy cream vanilla and powdered sugar until stiff. Spread over roll. Garnish with shaved chocolate. Slice and serve.

Makes 8-10 servings

Oven: 350°F   Bake Time: 15-20 min.

▤Passover Recipe

Matzo Apple Soufflé (D or P)

Nancy Simkin

6 matzos
water

6 eggs, separated
4 tart apples, grated
2/3 cup sugar
pinch salt
1/2 teaspoon cinnamon
1/2 cup walnuts
2 Tablespoons grated orange zest

4 Tablespoons butter or margarine
cinnamon and sugar for top

1. Soak matzos in cold water until soft. Drain well but do not press out water.
2. Beat egg whites until stiff. Set aside.
3. Beat matzo with egg yolks until smooth.
4. Add grated apples, sugar, salt, cinnamon, walnuts and orange zest. Mix well.
5. Fold beaten egg whites into matzo mixture.
6. Pour into well-greased 2 1/2-quart dish. Dot with butter and sprinkle with more cinnamon and sugar.
7. Bake at 350°F for about 1 hour.

Makes 4 to 6 servings

Oven: 350°F   Bake Time: 1 hour

▤Passover Recipe

✍ Recipe from my mother.

✓Good hot or cold.

Shirley's Rice Pudding (D)

Shirley Rutkovitz

2 eggs
1/2 cup sugar
1/4 teaspoon salt
2 cups milk, scalded
1/2 teaspoon vanilla
dash nutmeg
2 cups cooked rice
1/2 cup raisins

1. Put into mixing bowl eggs, sugar and salt. Beat well
2. Pour into egg mixture while stirring scalded milk, vanilla and nutmeg.
3. Mix in rice and raisins. Pour into greased 2-quart casserole dish. Bake at 350°F for 75 minutes, until a knife inserted close to the center comes out clean. Sprinkle top with nutmeg.

Makes 6 servings

Oven: 350°F   Bake Time: 1 hr. 15 min.

*D*ESSERTS

Rice Pudding (D)

Carisse Gafni

2 eggs
1 1/2 cups milk
1 1/2 cups cooked rice
1/3 cup packed brown sugar
1/4 teaspoon salt
1 teaspoon vanilla
1/4 teaspoon nutmeg

1. Preheat oven to 350°F.
2. Beat eggs. Add milk and beat until frothy.
3. Add all remaining ingredients. Mix well. Pour into greased 1 1/2-quart baking dish. Bake at 350°F for 70 minutes, until knife inserted in middle comes out clean.

Makes about 4 servings

Oven: 350°F   Bake Time: 70 min.

Pecan Pie (D)

Lori Lacey

9-inch piecrust
2 cups pecans
4 eggs
1 cup dark corn syrup
1/2 cup sugar
1/4 cup melted butter
1 teaspoon vanilla

1. Cover bottom of pie crust with pecans.
2. Beat eggs and blend in one ingredient at a time: corn syrup, sugar, butter and vanilla. Mix thoroughly.
3. Pour mixture over pecans and bake at 350°F for about one hour. Cool before serving.

Makes 1, 9-inch pie

Macaroon Sherbet Frozen Dessert (D)

Lori Lacey

18 (1-inch diameter) coconut macaroons, finely crushed
1 teaspoon vanilla extract
1/2 cup to 1 cup chopped walnuts
1 pint whipping cream, whipped
1 pint lemon sherbet, softened
1 pint lime sherbet, softened
1 pint raspberry sherbet, softened

1. Fold crushed macaroons, vanilla and chopped walnuts into whipped cream.
2. Spread half of the mixture into a 13x9x2-inch baking pan.
3. Alternately, place scoops of lemon, lime and raspberry sherbet over the mixture. Level with spatula.
4. Top with remaining whipped cream mixture.
5. Freeze until firm. Cut into squares. Enjoy!

Makes 12 to 15 servings

▤Passover Recipe

DESSERTS

Almond Float (D)

Linda Kutten

2 envelopes unflavored gelatin
1 cup water
2 cups milk
2/3 cup sugar
1 teaspoon almond extract
1 can (11 oz.) mandarin oranges
1 can (15 oz.) litchi
1 mango, cubed

1. Mix gelatin in cold water to soften gelatin.
2. Heat milk and sugar to simmering, do not boil.
3. Add softened gelatin mixture and almond extract. Stir to melt gelatin.
4. Pour into 9x9-inch pan. Refrigerate 3 to 4 hours to set. Chill fruit.
5. Cut gelled mixture into bite-size cubes.
6. Place chilled, drained fruits in bottom of large bowl. Place cubes on top and serve.

Makes 12 to 15 servings

▤Passover Recipe

✓For a dramatic presentation, make individual servings in a glass bowl and garnish with mint leaf or a sprig of rosemary.

✓Litchi is best fresh but very difficult to get. Hence we resort to canned litchi that is convenient as it is already peeled and pitted.

✓If you are unable to get litchi or mango, substitute with grapes and peaches.

▤Litchi is fruit native of southeastern Asia. It has a rough, red, leathery outer skin, an opaque white flesh and a brown shiny seed in the center. The white flesh is canned or dried. It is also known as litchee nut and lychee.

DESSERTS

MISCELLANEOUS

Dill Pickles (P)

Debbie Pomeranz

Pickling cucumbers
Quart jars
Dill

For each jar
1 and 1/2 bay leaf
5 and 2 peppercorns
1 red chili pepper
1 clove garlic
1 1/2 Tablespoons Kosher salt

1. Gently scrub pickling cucumbers.
2. On the bottom of each hot sterilized quart jar place dill to cover bottom. Add 1 bay leaf, 5 peppercorns, 1 red chili pepper, and 1 clove garlic.
3. Pack cucumbers in tightly to top of jar.
4. Put more dill on top, plus 2 more pepper corns, 1/2 bay leaf and 1 1/2 Tablespoon Kosher salt.
5. Fill with cold water. Seal tightly. Refrigerate. Ready in 2 weeks.

Aging time: 2 weeks

▤Passover Recipe

✍This recipe was passed down from Louis Dickens and Mary Garfinkle. Jake Garfinkle was famous for his home-grown cucumbers that went into this recipe.

Taiglach (P)

Adrienne Tropp

Dough
2 cups flour
1/4 teaspoon baking powder
1 Tablespoon sugar
1/2 teaspoon ground ginger
3 eggs
2 Tablespoons vegetable oil
1/2 teaspoon lemon zest
1/2 cup dates, halved
1/3 cup walnuts

Syrup
1 1/4 cup honey
1 cup sugar
2 teaspoons ground ginger
2 Tablespoons water

3 to 4 cups finely chopped walnuts or pecans
dried fruits to your liking (dates, apricots, etc.) or
candied fruits (cherries, pineapples, etc.)

1. *For dough*: Mix together flour, baking powder, sugar and ginger. Set aside. In food processor beat eggs. Beat in oil and zest. Add dates and walnuts. Process to chop fine. Pulse in flour mixture, to make soft dough. Divide dough into 3 balls. Roll into 1-inch diameter ropes. Slice 1/2-inch thick. Roll each slice into a ball. Set aside.
2. *Syrup*: In a 4 1/2-quart pot boil honey and sugar. Lower heat to a slow boil. Drop dough pieces in one at a time. Cover and cook over medium-low for 30 minutes. Do not uncover during this time as the dough needs to rise.
3. After 30 minutes, uncover. Gently stir. Use a soft silicone spoon or spatula to prevent breaking balls. Cover and cook until all are golden brown, about another 30 minutes.

Stir a few times during this cooking to brown evenly.

4. Mix ginger and water. Sprinkle over balls. Stir gently. Pour balls and syrup onto platter that has been rinsed with cold water. Keep pieces separated. Using food-handler gloves, pick up balls, roll in nuts and stack in a pyramid. The gloves allow you to handle the hot balls. After all the balls are coated there will be syrup left over. Roll dried or candied fruits in left over syrup then in nuts, add to stack.

Makes about 50 pieces of candy

Cook Time: about 1 hour

✡Taiglach is a traditional candy for Rosh Hashanah.

Easy Fudge (D)

Shirley Rutkovitz

1/4 cup butter or margarine
1 jar (7 oz) marshmallow cream
1 1/2 cups sugar
1 small can (7 fl. oz.) evaporated milk
1 bag (12 oz.) milk chocolate chips
1 teaspoon vanilla extract
1/2 cup to 1 cup chopped or broken nut meats

1. In a large saucepan (I have one pan I use only for this fudge), add butter, marshmallow, sugar, and evaporated milk. Boil 5 minutes, stirring constantly.
2. Remove from heat and immediately add chocolate chips and vanilla. Stir until chips are melted. Add nuts. Pour into lightly greased 8x8-inch pan. Cool.

Makes about 64, 1-inch pieces

Cranberry Fudge (D)

Pam Sloan

MISCELLANEOUS

12 ounces white chips
7 ounces marshmallow crème fluff, may substitute 2
    cups mini-marshmallows
1 cup craisins
1/2 teaspoon orange extract
1/3 cup evaporated milk
2 1/2 cups sugar
1/3 cup cranberry juice concentrate
1/4 cup butter

1. Line a 9x9-inch pan with aluminum foil and set aside.
2. Place white chips, marshmallow cream, craisins and orange extract into bowl.
3. In heavy 3-quart saucepan, heat milk on Medium until warm then add sugar. Bring to a rolling boil on Medium-High, stirring constantly with a wooden spoon. Reduce flame to still maintain the boil for 4 minutes. Add cranberry juice. Bring back to boil, boil for another 4 minutes to 235°F on the candy thermometer.
4. Remove from heat and add butter. Stir quickly until melted, 30 seconds.
5. Pour hot mixture over white chips mixture in bowl, without scraping the sides of the hot saucepan. Mix thoroughly until chips are melted. Pour into prepared pan. Cool at room temperature then chill in refrigerator.
6. Remove from pan; remove foil, cut into squares.

✓Cranberry Juice Concentrate is packed in a 12 oz. can, like a soda can. You may substitute frozen cranberry juice mix, thaw and use 1/3 cup.

✓Adding the cranberry juice in the middle of the total 8-minute boil is an easier way to adjust the boil time without getting complicated. Boil for 4 minutes; add the cranberry juice, the boil usually stops from 1 to 4 minutes, once boiling again start timing 4 minutes.

Jalapeno Jelly (P)

Pam Sloan

3/4 cup jalapeno (or serrano) peppers
2 medium green peppers, seeded and sliced
1 1/2 cups white vinegar
6 1/2 cups sugar
1 bottle (6 oz.) liquid pectin
1 Tablespoon dried red pepper flakes
green food coloring, optional

1. Place jalapeno peppers, green peppers, and vinegar in bowl of food processor with metal blade. Finely grind peppers with quick on and off turns.
2. Scrape pepper mixture into heavy saucepan. Stir in sugar. Cook over High, stirring constantly, until liquid comes to a full, rolling boil. Boil for 10 minutes. Remove from heat.
3. Stir in liquid pectin, red pepper flakes, and 2 to 3 drops food coloring, if desired. Immediately pour into hot sterilized jars and vacuum seal.

Makes 4, half-pint jars

✓Generally used as a hors d'oeuvre with cream cheese on water biscuits.
✓You can also use it as a glaze for meats, game, and poultry or as an accompaniment to meats or game.

MISCELLANEOUS

New York Egg Cream (D)

Jewish Fest

3 to 4 pumps chocolate syrup
1/2 cup chilled milk
3/4 cup chilled carbonated water, seltzer

1. Pump chocolate syrup into tall glass.
2. Pour milk into glass and stir.
3. Pour in carbonated water and serve.

Makes 1 serving

✓Fox's U Bet®Syrup is the syrup of choice but the other brands will work. This is just the syrup used in soda fountains of old.

✓Be sure the ingredients are well chilled, ice cold, it is best.

✓The above proportions are just suggestions. Add more of less of any ingredient to suit your taste.

✓Some purist say, "No brown head". This means that the top should be pure white. Making it as above will result in a brown head. To make a white head place the milk and part of the seltzer in the glass, pour in the syrup, then the remainder of the seltzer. Do not stir, let the drinker enjoy the white head and do the stirring.

MENUS

Shabbat

Challah, p. 193-199
Honey-Mustard Chicken with Cashews, p. 133
Herbed Peas, p. 154
Potato Kugel, p. 162
Apple Cake, p. 236

Arielle, age 12

Rosh Hashanah

Sliced Apples with Honey
Round Challah, p. 193-199
Gefilte Fish
Chicken Soup with Matzo Balls, p. 86-88
Chopped Liver, p. 60-64
Brisket, p. 105-114
Tsimmes, p. 153
Noodle Kugel, p. 164-165
Rugalach, p. 212

Yom Kippur – Kol Nidre Prefast Dinner

Round Challah, p. 193-199
Chicken Soup with Kreplach, p. 84, 86-87
Chicken with Orange-Pecan Rice, p. 132
Honeyed Baby Carrots, p. 152
Honey Chiffon Cake, p. 229

Yom Kippur - Break the Fast Menu

Bagels & Lox with Cream Cheese
Sliced Tomatoes, Onion
Noodle Kugel, p. 165
Sour Cream Coffee Cake, p. 188

Sukkot

Challah served with Honey, p. 193-199
Veggie Soup, p. 81
Stuffed Cabbage, p. 120-121
Sole Amandine on a Bed of Vegetables, p. 146
Fruit Strudel, p. 256

Simchat Torah

Challah with Honey, p. 193-199
Hearty Lentil Soup, p. 82
Honey Curry Chicken, p. 124
Carrot Kugel, p. 161
Lemon Squares, p. 227

Hanukkah

Chicken Soup with Matzoh Balls, p. 86-88
Potato Latkes with Applesauce, p. 175-176
Kasha Varniskes, p. 157-158
Cranberry Chicken, p. 128
Sufganiyot, p. 201

Tu B'Shevat

Mushroom Barley Soup, p. 80
Whole Wheat Challah, p. 199
Pineapple Brisket, p. 113
Yam Casserole, p. 156
Date Nut Bread, p. 191

Purim

Stuffed Cabbage, p. 120-121
Roasted Lemon Chicken, p. 123
Couscous with Apricots, p. 95
Lemon Poppy Seed Cookies. p. 223
Hamantaschen, p. 203-207

MENUS

Passover

Chicken Soup with Matzo Balls, p. 86-88
Matzo served with Charoset, p. 47-50
Chicken Breasts with Matzo-Farfel Stuffing, p. 126
Steamed Vegetables
Macaroons with Sherbet, p. 217
Chocolate Matzo, p. 213-214

Shavuot

Challah (2), p. 193-199
Fruit Compote, p. 75-76
Cheese Blintzes, p. 181-183
Pesto Crusted Salmon, p. 141
Savory Potato Kugel, p. 163
New York Cheesecake, p. 253
Milk

Jonathan, age 10

Index

INDEX

INDEX

INDEX

INDEX

INDEX

INDEX

INDEX

INDEX

INDEX

INDEX

INDEX

INDEX

INDEX

How to Order

Get additional copies of this cookbook by returning the order form and your check or money order to:

Temple Sinai Cookbook
Temple Sinai
3405 Gulling Road
Reno, NV 89503

Please send me _____ copies of **40 Years in the Desert Temple Sinai Cookbook** at **$20.00** per copy and **$5.00** for shipping and handling per book. Enclosed is my check or money order for $_____.

Mail Books To:

Name: _____

Address:_____

City: _____

State: _____ Zip: _____
Phone Number: (Just in case we need to get in touch with you concerning the order)
(_____) _____

If you have a question call Temple Sinai at 775-747-5508 or email Temple.Sinai@Juno.com

ORDER FORM

40 Years
in the Desert
Temple Sinai Cookbook

All proceeds from the cookbook benefits Temple Sinai:
Temple Sinai Building Fund
Temple Sinai Religious School